Beauty for Ashes

The Miracle of Melanie Grimsley

Beauty for Ashes

The miracle of Melanie Grimsley

Ivan Little &
Melanie Grimsley

PUBLISHING

Award Publishing Northern Ireland
cedricwilson@live.co.uk

Award Publishing Northern Ireland
cedricwilson@live.co.uk

Typesetting by *www.wordzworth.com*

Dedication

In loving memory of Amanda Kathleen Grimsley
17/04/85 – 09/04/88
One day we will be together again

Contents

Roy Millar

As I looked at the two-year-old Melanie Grimsley in the Children's Hospital in Belfast in 1988 the future seemed bleak indeed. Just what kind of future could she possibly have?

Well, now we know. For in this book Melanie has invited us into her life - not just the outer event but the inner world where she has wrestled with deep questions of meaning, identity, and purpose. Her prose descriptions are sometimes heart rending and her poetry, written in moments of perplexity, is both profound and deeply moving.

This book is very important for a number of reasons. In the first place it is a testimony of hope. In the second place it is a timely challenge to some of the values of our contemporary western culture that often seems drowned in a sea of triviality - the superficial issues of style and appearance and celebrity.

So if you have a taste for tragedy and triumph, poetry and pathos, romance and redemption, have a good read.

ROY MILLAR, MELANIE'S PLASTIC SURGEON

Bishop Ken Clarke

Melanie's story is one of the most remarkable I have read in a very long time. It is profoundly moving, totally gripping and genuinely inspirational. It is a story of deep pain, sudden shock, sustained resilience and raw faith. Here you will find disarming honesty and amazing courage. In a culture obsessed with appearance and trivia here is a story of true beauty and real depth. All I can say is this... What a girl! What a story! What a God! This is a must read!

BISHOP KEN CLARKE, CHURCH OF IRELAND
BISHOP OF KILMORE ELPHIN AND ARDAGH

Arlene Foster

Melanie Grimsley has real beauty. I admire this young woman so much for her strength, her bravery and her determination. Hers is also sadly a story of prejudice and bullying, of grief and heartache. But whilst those are the experiences which Melanie has faced you will finish this book with a smile on your face because it is also a story of succeeding against the odds, of determination, of discovery, of true bravery and most of all a story of love: the love of Melanie's parents for their little girl, the love which Brian and Melanie share and the love she now exhibits to her two boys.

I know you will enjoy this inspirational story and I'm so proud to be associated with it.

ARLENE FOSTER MLA

Simon Weston

I first met Melanie Grimsley in 1994 when she was a charming yet nervous girl who was still coming to terms with her injuries. It fills me with joy to see how far she has come. Through sheer determination, faith, courage and with the help of her family, she has built a life that is full of happiness. Her strength shines through along with a powerful message which, I am certain, will help others to overcome adversity of any kind.

SIMON WESTON OBE

An Introduction

by Ivan Little

Melanie Grimsley is a living, breathing miracle – a remarkable, courageous and resilient woman and mother who came within seconds of death in a horrific car fire which killed her sister on an unseasonably hot April day back in 1988.

Only for the selfless bravery of a man who plucked her from the inferno, Melanie would undoubtedly have perished along with her sister Amanda.

But Melanie, who had just turned two, didn't escape unscathed from the raging fire in the busy market town of Enniskillen in Northern Ireland.

The girl from the small Fermanagh village of Kesh sustained appalling injuries which left her badly disfigured. It took years of surgery to reconstruct her face and to give her digits on her hands which were virtually burned away in the fire which was front page news in papers and featured on television bulletins around the world.

The blaze broke out around 3pm on what was Grand National Day in 1988 after devoted mother Pamela Grimsley popped into a shop to buy milk, leaving her daughters Melanie and Amanda who was almost three in the family Austin Maestro car. It's a decision she's regretted ever since.

The pretty little girls were in their usual good form that day as they went into Enniskillen with their Mum to leave their visiting aunt at the bus depot. Amanda was wearing a pink blouse, pink pinafore and white socks while her younger sister looked resplendent in a white jumper, burgundy pinafore and white tights.

No-one knows for sure why the blaze started and even though there were dozens of theories, protracted investigations by the police, the fire service and independent experts have not been able to establish the precise cause.

A high-profile compensation case in Belfast's High Court was settled before the legal arguments about the reasons for the fire were heard.

What is certain, however, is that Melanie Grimsley is lucky to be alive. And she owes her life to her rescuer Oliver Quinn whose heroism she acknowledged many years later when she named one of her sons after him.

What is also beyond doubt is that Melanie Grimsley is indebted to the medical teams who worked tirelessly to help the tragic toddler who has blossomed into an inspirational young woman.

Melanie has not only had to endure countless operations to give her a new face and hands but she has also had to steel herself to the cruelty of countless people who've stared at her, who've pointed at her, and who've even made cheap jibes about her behind her back – and to her face.

A lesser person might have crumbled under the pressure and the pain. And certainly Melanie had her bad times as she grew up.

In some ways, her life started all over again after she woke up in hospital after the fire. She didn't really remember the tragedy or what her life had been like before the blaze. She grew up in hospitals with medical professionals all around her. That was her normality.

But as well as the agonies of the non-stop surgery, there were also the bullies who made her formative years hell. Not forgetting the grief Melanie also suffered for Amanda, the sister she never really knew.

Added to that – the guilt of surviving the fire and the nagging questions which shook the foundations of the Christian beliefs which were instilled in her from an early age.

Yet Melanie Grimsley has emerged from her dark days as a shining light of hope and strength and her fears that her facial disfigurement would stop her enjoying a normal life have been totally dispelled.

Her parents' role in her recovery can't be over-stated. William and Pamela have been Melanie's towers of strength. Without them, she would never have got through her physical and mental ordeals. They never wavered and their determination to make life as normal as possible for Melanie has been the lynchpin of her life.

I remember hearing how Pamela and her twin buggy used to be regular fixtures on the streets of Kesh. And people used to think that Melanie and Amanda who was just eleven months older were actually twins. But after the fire William and Pamela resolved not to hide Melanie away.

She was barely recognisable as the cute two-year-old who had captivated so many folk with her smile. Some villagers simply couldn't bring themselves to look at Melanie. Some broke down in tears. But still, the Grimsleys persisted with their 'normalisation' campaign. And gradually it paid off.

They also tried to teach Melanie to ignore the people who stared at her or who walked out of restaurants because they didn't want to be seated near 'the little girl with the burns.'

But in her later life three other important people would emerge to play equally big roles in Melanie's life.

They are her loving husband Brian Higgins and their two sons William and Leo who simply see Melanie as the best Mum in the world.

But now Melanie has decided to tell her story. In "Beauty for Ashes – The Miracle of Melanie Grimsley" she talks movingly and openly about the impact of the fire and her sister's death on her life; about the days of despair when she thought she could no longer go on but she also shares the good times too.

Melanie hopes her story will be an example to other people that if she can emerge from her traumatic past to live a normal life, anyone can.

I first encountered Melanie after a chance meeting in 2005 with her father William who told me she was getting married and I followed up our chat with a formal request to Melanie for her approval to make a television documentary about her big day and her life story.

Melanie and her husband-to-be Brian Higgins agreed to co-operate and I met them for the first time in the town of Lisnaskea.

I would be a liar if I didn't admit that I was, initially, quite shocked by Melanie's facial injuries. But her engaging personality quickly won me over. And now whenever we meet, I never even notice her disfigurement. As her husband Brian says, you look beyond the injuries to see the real Melanie Grimsley/Higgins.

Through covering Northern Ireland's troubles for over 30 years for Ulster Television, Downtown Radio and the Belfast Telegraph, I thought I'd become numb to tragedy and immovable by the courage of inspirational survivors, dozens of whom it's been my privilege to meet.

But few interviewees have been quite like Melanie Grimsley. Her ordeal, her recovery, her upbeat attitude and her fortitude are quite astonishing. And I'm not alone in my admiration.

Later in the book, I tell the stories of the people who've helped and who've been helped by Melanie including her parents, her sisters, the man who saved her life and the medics who put her shattered life back together again.

If reading this incredibly courageous survivor's story is half as uplifting as writing about it, you're in for on amazing journey in Beauty for Ashes – The Miracle of Melanie Grimsley.

IVAN LITTLE
BELFAST, OCTOBER 2011

Chapter 1

Dreams, Nightmares and a Guardian Angel

Isaiah 61 v 3 (New Living Translation)
"....He will give them a crown of beauty for ashes"

I watch him sleeping, his little arms outstretched. His six teddy bears are lying all around him because he doesn't have the heart to leave any of them out of his bed.

A wave of love rushes over me as I put my hand on my pregnant tummy to feel my unborn baby kicking inside me to say goodnight to his brother.

I don't have long to go now, just another 11 weeks and my new little son will be here.

I smile as I imagine the two boys playing together at Christmas. And I laugh to myself as I wonder if William will want to bring his brother to bed along with his ever growing number of teddies.

But suddenly other darker thoughts come into my mind.

What would I do if anything happened to my beautiful babies? What if my time with them was limited? What if all this was taken away from me?

They may seem reasonable enough worries for any young mother because as soon as anyone finds out they're guarding a little life inside them, the instinct to love and protect becomes overwhelming.

But I can't help thinking of another young mother with her two children on a spring evening over 20 years earlier.

As she tucked her little girls up in bed – beside their teddy bears – on Friday, April 8, 1988 she could never have imagined what the next day had in store for them. A day which would change their lives – and their entire world – for ever.

80C3

I don't remember much about any of that Saturday afternoon, of course. I was only two years old and I think the mind can block out the memories which are just too painful to recall.

It's probably a blessing that I don't have to live with those memories, those images of a day that has left a legacy which I will never be able to forget.

Physical scars are hard to heal and hard to recover from. But there is treatment for them. Scars left on your mind and your heart stay with you for a lifetime.

Amanda was just eight days away from her third birthday. I had just turned two a few weeks earlier.

For our Mum, Pamela, I'm sure it was like a day's work in itself getting us out of the house and into the car. We travelled from our home in Kesh to Enniskillen to leave our Auntie Stephanie – Mum's sister- to the bus station. She was returning to Birmingham in England that afternoon after a family visit.

Mum must have been exhausted and was probably looking forward to a cup of tea the moment she got back to Kesh. Maybe that's what reminded her that we had no milk in the house. And that's why she stopped at Rooney's shop on the Cornagrade Road in Enniskillen.

She left me and my sister in the car, knowing she'd be back in a couple of minutes. I don't blame Mum. As a young mother myself now, I know that bringing two toddlers into a shop can be a major challenge.

By the time a mother battles with their seats and tries to explain to her children why they can't have all the sweets they see in front of them in the shop, she could have been in and out of the place twice over.

And besides, how much can go wrong inside just a few minutes?

Mum was paying for her milk on that sunny Saturday afternoon when she heard a commotion outside.

She looked out and saw billowing smoke. I can't possibly imagine what she must have felt as she realised it was her car – our car – which was on fire.

No-one has ever discovered exactly why the car – an Austin Maestro – went on fire. All sorts of possible causes have been advanced but what is certain is that it didn't take long for the car to be engulfed by flames.

And that is why I'm glad I don't remember a thing about the blaze. I don't remember what I saw or what I thought was happening or what I did.

All I know is that it would have been a terrifying ordeal for a grown-up, never mind a two year old girl. And I know I wouldn't be alive today but for what happened next in the frightening and frantic moments after the unstoppable fire took hold.

I don't know if I even noticed the hand of the stranger coming into the blazing car to try to grab my burning body.

I'm told I was rolled on the grass in a bid to extinguish the flames. Doubtless, I was in shock, unaware of anything that was going on around me.

But my rescuer hadn't finished. He attempted to save Amanda but she was beyond his reach and the fire was gaining in intensity.

He fought hard to save Amanda and he didn't want to give up, despite sustaining burns himself. I don't know where he got his strength from. Or his courage as he risked his life to save other lives. Ultimately, he was beaten back by the flames and Amanda died.

But I owe my life to that man. His name is Oliver Quinn and he tells his own story later in the book But I thank God that I was so fortunate to have had someone so selfless and so brave passing my way that day.

I don't believe his presence outside the shops that day was an accident. Oliver was my guardian angel and there is no doubt that without him I would not be here now.

People often call me brave but I argue that I had no choice.

Oliver had a choice. He could have called an ambulance and the fire brigade and simply waited for them to arrive.

But no, Oliver didn't think twice about the obvious dangers or give way to the shock and panic which must have consumed him as he saw the harrowing scene in front of him.

He reached into the car with his hands of hope and they offered me a second chance at life.

Oliver was able to say that I was in the front part of the car. Yet when Mum went into the shop my sister and I had been in the back, in our seats.

No-one, least of all me of course, can explain how I got from the back of the car into the front, or even what made me do so. It's just one of a series of unresolved mysteries from a dreadful and disastrous day – a day which saw the tragic loss of my beloved sister and a miraculous escape for me.

It's a day that has taken me all of my life so far to come to terms with.

I'm told a passing driver took me to the Erne hospital in Enniskillen where I was given immediate medical assistance but the staff there don't specialise in the treatment of burns. So I was rushed in an ambulance the 90 miles to the Royal Belfast Hospital for Sick Children.

I don't know what must have been going through the minds of my Mum and my Dad, William at that time. I often look at my own little boys and I just can't imagine the magnitude of the pain I would feel if either of them became seriously ill. Or even worse.

Not only did my parents have to deal with their loss but they also had me, lying barely recognisable in a hospital. They didn't know if I would live or die.

And the truth is they didn't know which of those outcomes would be worse.

For looking at me then few people thought I would have had much of a life ahead of me such was the scale of the massive injuries which had been inflicted on me.

But we had all suffered a massive loss with Amanda's passing. And the Grimsley family also lost the life we once had. We also lost a part of ourselves. And we lost the certainty of tomorrow.

No-one knew what lay ahead any more.

But my parents resolved that we would now take each day as it came. We had a mountain to climb. And all we had to do that was each other.

Little did I know then that although I had lost so much, I would also gain love, support and encouragement that would give me the strength of spirit and the determination to get me through and make me who I am today.

And so began the first day of the rest of my life. And the only way to go now was forward. Because there was simply no going back.

At the outset, there was a period when doctors didn't hold out much hope for me.

But happily I did survive and the burns to my face, head and arms were particularly extensive. Yet the initial time in hospital isn't one I can recall with any clarity.

My earliest memories are from about a year after the accident. I knew I had to go to hospital because I had burns and I could tell people the rudimentary details in simple childish terms if they ever asked me about everything.

But I don't think I really understood the full extent of what they were doing for me. And to me.

Initially I had to receive skin grafts. The skin was taken from other parts of my body – the donor sites they called them - which hadn't been burnt. And that skin was grafted onto the burnt areas.

Now all that was especially painful. Doubly painful in fact because the donor sites had to recover at the same time as the healing of the areas to which the skin had been grafted.

There were other major problems too.

I'd also lost my fingers and reconstructive surgery was needed. And my facial features almost all completely disappeared after the fire.

I have seen a television news report about me not long after the accident. The interviewer asked me why I was going to hospital. And I replied "They are going to make me new fingers"

It's funny looking at it now. I was only three years old at the time and my answer was delivered in a laidback tone of voice as if the procedure was no big deal – something that was an ordinary everyday occurrence.

Obviously, I was totally oblivious to how much work it would actually take, how extraordinary it all was.

My hands were little stumps with all the fingers fused together and the doctors worked on them for eight years to create the fingers I have now.

They separated them one by one using skin and tissue from other parts of my body to mould them. My hands are small and my fingers end where other adults' second knuckle is.

As a result my hands are the size of children's hands.

Down the years I've often said that I hate my hands. But when I think about it now I realise they are actually amazing. And I am lucky to have fingers at all.

As for the rest of the surgery, I also had repeated operations to reconstruct my ears, eyes, nose and mouth.

I was a regular visitor to hospital operating theatres. But I can recall one time when instead of bringing me in on several different occasions, my surgeons decided to do all the procedures together.

They reckoned it would be less stressful emotionally and physically for me to get it all done at once rather than having to keep going up and down to theatre.

The operation lasted over six hours, with work on all areas of my face, my hands and also on the wounds on my legs from which skin had been taken for my grafts.

It was less stressful but I still have no idea how I coped with it all. Remember I was only around seven years old by that stage. I was due to be starting my first day at a new school. But instead I had to go into hospital. Again. And again.

I think the worry of feeling left out from - and left behind by - the rest of the class was nearly more devastating than the surgery itself. I can clearly remembering crying all the way to Belfast.

Another thing I detested was wearing a plastic mask which had been made for me to wear on my face. Layer upon layer of cream was put on underneath to smooth out my skin.

In retrospect, I'm glad that my parents persisted with it and made sure I wore it. Now that I'm older I know how it reduced my scars down from their swollen state. It flattened them and smoothed them.

The medical teams were wonderful. And they even agreed to my requests to make a mask like mine for my doll! The surgeons, I know, still have a laugh about that doll, even to this day.

But I just loved having a little someone just like me – a mini-me. A mini-Melanie!

On reflection, my experiences showed that children do have an astonishing ability to adapt to their situations, no matter how difficult. As I grew up that is what I did. This was my life and it was the only life I knew. So I just got on with it.

I can now see that it is in my nature to be determined. And as a young child, it was a quality that I needed in abundance. I had to be determined otherwise I would have not have made it through those long and traumatic years.

Of course, hospitals have come a long way from my initial visits. They're now more child-orientated with toys and play specialists in the wards and in the theatres.

But I used to be scared – and I still am.

When I was little and going to theatre, I dreaded the anaesthetic room and being held on the operating table with a black mask on my face.

Because my hands and arms were so badly burned, they couldn't put needles into them. So they had to give me injections in my feet.

It never got any easier and as I say, the fears still haunt me.

As a young child I didn't see the point of the operations. I just wanted to be left alone. I didn't understand how crucial the operations were.

I didn't appreciate that if my eyes were not operated on the skin would be too tight to allow my eyes to close during my sleep and my eyes would dry out.

I didn't realise that if the skin on my hands and arms was not released as my body grew then I would no longer be able to stretch them and they would become restricted.

No, the way I saw it was that I kept going into hospital, only to come out looking the same.

To me, the surgery didn't make me look any better or change anything. People still stared. I still stood out. I still struggled to do things with my hands.

So why bother with all the surgery?

And I hated being different. I resented hospital and the aftermath of the surgery.

For while I was in there and recovering from the operations, normal life was going on as usual for everyone else.

That was all I wanted – a normal life. Only it wasn't to be. For a long time to come.

My Mum used to come down to theatre with me and she told me she would stay with me. But as I got older it was Dad who always came with me.

6

Because Mum found it increasingly difficult to cope. Only now that I'm a parent myself can I fully understand how she must have felt.

My lack of understanding about what was happening around me made it hard for anyone to try and explain the situation to me. All I wanted to do was to go home.

Nowadays, I only have to think about my own little boys to imagine what my parents were going through in those early days.

And I remember the anguish I felt as my son William endured a particularly bad nappy rash when he was about a year old. William screamed as we bathed him and I had tears in my eyes as I tried not to hurt him while I was putting on cream to soothe the rash.

The pain lasted only a few days. But for my Mum and Dad, it was a constant nightmare, with little or no respite.

I often had to be put in the bath to remove difficult dressings. Sometimes it was too much for all of us and my parents would take me to theatre to redress my wounds. One vivid memory is the time Dad and I counted the stitches as the medical staff were taking them out. I'm not sure now exactly how many there were but I do remember counting up to EIGHTY of them.

In the early days when I was in hospital in Belfast, my parents used to stay with my Dad's sister Myrtle who lived in the city. They wanted to be close to me as the travelling between Fermanagh and Belfast was too long to make on a daily basis.

For the first few months at least any idea of leading a normal life was simply impossible.

This was our life now.

And so it went on. Operations followed operations throughout my early years on a regular basis. I once asked Mum how I continued to develop and if I learnt just like any other two year old. Mum laughed and said 'Mel, those nurses taught you everything you know.'

By the time I was three or four years old, I really don't think I noticed my burns any longer. Not in the way that everyone else did anyway.

To me, I was just me.

And there is something about that child-like acceptance, that freedom that I long to have back.

I had no hair so I just wore a hat.

I had burns. But it wasn't my fault. So I just carried on as normally as I could. But in reality it was more difficult for my parents around that time because every time we went somewhere new, the heads would turn. And people would stare at me.

Mum told me she loved going into our local village, Kesh, because it was the one place no-one looked at me or asked what had happened to me.

However like most other children, I did want to go swimming and I did want to go to the park. But they presented their own peculiar problems. For they were the places where children gathered in huge numbers.

Mum and Dad might well have said no to my requests to go here there and everywhere. They could have turned down my pleas, blaming the stress that outings could cause to me and to them. They could have said they wanted to spare me from having to deal with all the looks, all the finger pointing and all the stares, not to mention the behind-back whisperings and gossiping. But they didn't succumb and take the easy option.

No, they held their heads up high and instilled in me a sense of pride and self-worth. They taught me that I had to accept who I was. They told me if anyone had a problem with me it was their problem and not mine.

More than once they insisted that I had as much right as anyone else to go out. And their philosophy hit home with me. And it still does because I never ever forget the invaluable advice that my parents imparted to me.

I recently read a newspaper article published not long after the accident and which had the headline "We are not ashamed of Melanie. We will not hide her away."

That was how my parents decided to treat me from day one. And that is the attitude I adopted too.

Chapter 2

Learning Lessons and Teaching the Doubters that I Could Stand on My Own Two Feet

I could hardly wait to start school. I was keen to go along with everyone else my age to Kesh Primary School.

I was determined that I was not going to be held back and I wanted to be treated just like every one of the near 200 pupils in the school. My mum still laughs about me when I was little because she would try to tell me that things might sometimes be different because I was 'special'.

My response was defiant. "I don't want to be special" I told her in no uncertain terms, apparently.

Certainly, there were aspects of my schooling which did require special consideration and attention. For a start, I needed time off for my repeated hospital visits and rehabilitation.

But there was absolutely nothing wrong with my ability to learn and I was allowed to attend the mainstream school. But there were subtle little differences, decisions which were made for me but which made me feel really excluded from my peers.

I was doing a talk recently for the local Women's Institute group and one of my primary school teachers who was present was really honest with me afterwards.

She recalled that at the open day at school for the new P1 class, she was dubious after I insisted I wanted to paint.

She looked at my hands and wondered how I could paint a picture and how I would feel in front of the other children if I couldn't do as well as them. She said she reluctantly gave me a paintbrush. But she was surprised when I completed what she had to admit was the best painting in the class.

That in a nutshell summed up what my entire time had been like at school. I almost felt that I had something to prove to everyone else.

I had to be the same as the rest of the pupils. I didn't want to be special or different so I had to work hard to make sure I wasn't.

I learned to write along with everyone else and because my hands are the only hands I have ever known I just learned to do it my own way. I think it must be harder to have to re-learn skills after you've become accustomed to doing things with full sized hands. But I just got on with it the best I could.

I had a classroom assistant in primary school to help me do things, such as changing my shoes for going outside and I also got assistance for arts and crafts. And there was also help for me after I came out of hospital after my numerous surgeries there.

But to be blunt, I hated having that classroom assistant. The very fact that I had one seemed to threaten my independence. It suggested that I couldn't cope before I'd even tried to cope. And I often got upset about the decision that I should have one.

Although I had to take time out away from my studies to go to hospital I never got behind in my schoolwork and I was always in the top groups in my class. As I say, I think I had a determination and a desire to prove I could do anything I wanted, despite my burns.

I remember in my early years at school everyone seemed very protective of me. But again that frustrated me as I was trying to be like everyone else and resented feeling smothered.

I also loathed break-time at school when everyone went outside to play football. Cheers would erupt from the playground as another goal was scored and the triumphant team would laugh and congratulate themselves on winning. I stood and watched from the edge of the grass, my classroom assistant by my side. That was as far as I could go. I still don't know why I couldn't join in. All I was ever told was that I couldn't play in case I got hurt.

Everyone else joined in. So I was on my own. And it was that isolation which hurt.

People question how much a child actually understands at early age but I knew that I was different. And that exclusion from my peer group only reinforced my belief that I wasn't like everyone else, no matter how hard I tried to be just like them.

I often wondered how my class could ever accept me when the rules that were in place prevented them from doing just that.

Eventually, however, the restrictions were lifted. Maybe it was my incessant questioning of 'why not' that finally saw me getting the go-ahead to take part, though I will never forget my debut, my first day at football.

The kids in my class decided I should be in goals, probably due to their lack of faith in my ability to play in an outfield position.

I hadn't really got a clue about what I should be doing in nets. But as the ball came hurtling towards me, I just reacted instinctively and kicked it straight up towards the other end of the pitch.

I remember everyone came running towards me, telling me I had saved a goal. They were all so happy with me. I had done well. I was part of the team.

I don't remember if we won the game that day and it didn't matter because for the first time in my life I felt like everyone else.

From that day forward I knew I didn't have to stand on the side-lines and watch other people. I didn't have to be apart from the crowd. I could join in, be part of society and be accepted.

I also took up horse-riding. Which again came as a surprise to many people who didn't expect me to be able to do it.

I'd been invited along to the local Riding for the Disabled group one morning when I was around five-years-old and I really enjoyed it and looked forward to getting out of school for a few hours on a Thursday morning.

I loved my horse and I loved hearing - for the very first time in my life - someone telling me I COULD do something rather than being told that I COULDN'T do it. I felt empowered and I will always be thankful to the RDA group for focusing on my ability rather than my disability and for nurturing in me a sense of self belief and a 'can do' attitude.

They helped me to build on the positive attitude that my parents had always encouraged me to have.

It had always been other people who limited me and sadly it happened all over again when I was eight-years-old and wanted to play the violin.

We all had to sit a music test to see who could go for lessons as spaces were limited. I'd always enjoyed music and had been taking piano lessons. So I flew through the test and got the top marks in my class. I was so excited because I had a guaranteed place in the violin class. Or so I thought.

The music tutor told me that even though I came out tops in the test, it had been decided there'd be no sense in teaching me the violin as my hands would stop me progressing very far.

I totally objected to the decree. I may have been just a child but I could see the injustice of their decision. They'd written me off without giving me a chance.

Stubbornly, I wouldn't settle for that.

As usual with all my complaints about my treatment in life, I told my parents over and over again how wrong it was. In the end the school gave in and they had no option but to let me try the violin.

I enjoyed learning how to play and proving people wrong. That is what mattered. But yes, I did give it up when it all got too much for me.

Before that however, our school was chosen to appear on the Ulster Television programme 'School around the Corner' which was hosted by Frank Mitchell. It was a big moment for Kesh Primary to be selected as one of the schools from the country to appear on the show.

Our violin group was picked to play on the programme. And naturally, we were all nervous because we wanted to play the best we had ever performed. We busied ourselves practising. And when the big day came and the cameras started to roll, I smiled as I proudly held my violin – the violin they said I couldn't play.

In that very moment, I think I really did shine. A new string had been added to my bow....

Chapter 3

My Day in Court...but Nothing Could Compensate Me for Hating Myself

I walked up and down the marble floors of the cavernous Courts of Justice building in the centre of Belfast, quietly impressed at the noise my shoes made as I skipped up and down.

I didn't pass any remarks on the fact I was the only one there making any noise at all. Or that it might have been totally inappropriate in the circumstances.

But I was tired of the toy pony that I brought to amuse myself. And the little box of Tic-tac's weren't doing much to ease my hunger.

No, I was convinced that this place was – apart from church – the most boring spot I'd ever been.

We went to the court on Monday, January 10, 1994 for the hearing of the compensation case on which lawyers had been working for so long.

I was only about seven years old and I didn't understand why I was there or what was going on. My recollections of it all are scant.

But I do remember the humiliation of having to show my scars on my face, hands and body to a room full of strangers. I felt like the centrepiece of an exhibition.

I didn't know how they were going to assess what I'd been through or what I would go through for the rest of my life just by looking at me.

There was more to it than that of course. But all I knew was that I'd been in a car with my Mum and Amanda which had gone on fire. And it shouldn't have.

Because of the nature of the legal system I had to sue my parents and their insurance company for compensation. The case was brought through my uncle Ian, my Daddy's brother.

I also sued the Erne Engineering Company who sold the car to Dad and T.P. Topping of Enniskillen who serviced the Maestro.

Everyone denied liability.

Newspaper cuttings of the first day of the case show that my barrister Mr Mervyn Morrow QC told the court the fire authorities and forensic experts had been unable to find the cause of the blaze.

But Mr Morrow said it was caused by the courtesy light. He said the light went on and off for no apparent reason and that was consistent with a loose connection which created a "hot spot."

The full details of the hearing are set out in a later chapter of the book but on day two of the proceedings the case was settled 'out of court.' I was told by my lawyers that a settlement had been reached. But I really didn't have a clue about the legalities.

I was however relieved that my Mum had been spared the ordeal of having to go into the witness box to give evidence.

I know now that she would undoubtedly have been subjected to distressing questions about the fire. I've always said – and I'll say it again - that she wasn't to blame in any shape or form for the blaze.

In the court that day, a confidentiality clause was agreed and that means I can't reveal the amount of compensation I received. And it limits me from saying too much about my feelings about the legal system.

After the case was over and we went outside the court, Dad told reporters that there should be a 'no fault' system for compensating injured children.

My Dad explains his thinking in the second half of the book but I know that he is still angry about the whole process.

I think he, like everyone else in my family, had hoped that the cause of the fire would finally be revealed during the High Court case which had been expected to last a couple of weeks.

Dad is convinced that the courtesy light was to blame for the blaze but because a settlement was agreed, what evidence there was about that and all the other theories, was never aired and analysed in open court.

Essentially, the fire is still as big a mystery today as it was in April 1988.

Obviously, in reaching the settlement, the lawyers were all doing their best for me in very difficult and trying circumstances, but sometimes I wonder what would have emerged if the case had run its full course.

For me, the lingering frustration is that the cause of the fire wasn't established. The probability is that it never will. And I will never know what caused Amanda's death – and my terrible injuries.

Would it be easier if I did know? I'm not sure.

We all search for answers, for logic and for reason - something that can help us put together the broken pieces. But sadly for the Grimsley family, we never got the vital responses to the questions which still hang over the fire.

And that is what bothers me much more than money.

I also back my Dad in his calls for a 'no fault' system of compensation. In today's society where people get damages without question for everything and anything, it seems strange that a case like ours had to go the way it did after nearly six years of preparation.

I don't know the ins and outs of my lengthy legal battle. But I don't believe that my search for answers – or closure - was resolved with that court settlement back in 1994.

The papers in the files about my case run to tens of thousands of pages. And my legal team have given them to me – with a health warning.

My solicitor cautioned me, as a friend not as a lawyer, that I should think carefully before reading the files. I think he was concerned that some of the information contained in them could upset me.

I wasn't ready to peruse the papers back then. I still haven't read them. And I don't know if I ever will.

But the sad reality is that the answers which I'm still seeking about the fire probably aren't in there. Or else they would have come out during the proceedings.

Even though I've never read them, I know that it's important for me to have the files in my possession because they are part of me. They are my past. But I won't let them ruin my future.

Despite everything back then in the court and in the hospital, I was progressing well. My operations were all going according to plan. And academically I was always in the top group of my class. Yes, on the surface everything appeared to be going well. But inside I was struggling.

I just felt so different from everyone else. My self-esteem was at rock bottom. I thought I was ugly. And I resented how I looked.

It's fair to say I hated myself.

One day I was deeply upset as I returned home from school. All the other girls in my class had been cast in the roles of angels in the Nativity play. Me? I was asked to be a Christmas tree.

It transpired the reason why they wanted me play the part was because it was a speaking role and I was a clear speaker. I thought it was because I wasn't pretty enough to be an angel like the other girls. My Mum told me she would make the most beautiful Christmas tree outfit anyone had ever seen. But that didn't pacify me. I was just too hurt…and it's all a telling reminder of how I felt about myself. Never good enough. Never up there with everyone else.

My heartache was compounded by the fact that I still missed Amanda. After the accident, Mum had two more daughters Elaine and Bethany. And although I love them dearly there was still a gap in my life.

Obviously I was too young to have vivid memories of Amanda as she was. But still there was something missing. I also had to live with the fact that I'd escaped from the car. But Amanda didn't and she died. And looking back on that now, I realise that even as a child I felt guilty. Survivor guilt, I think they call it now.

I can clearly remember at the age of five or six I cried myself to sleep every night. During the day I kept my thoughts in check. But there was something about the dark quietness of the night that let them flow openly.

I kept my demons to myself. I never talked about them to anyone; I didn't want to burden anyone, especially my parents. I could see how upset I made them. I wanted to do well. I wanted to cope with everything. I wanted to make my parents proud of me.

Everyone told me how brave I was. And I didn't want to disappoint. But as I said earlier I never believed I was brave. I didn't have a choice. And that started to frustrate me.

Behind my outwardly show of resilience and determination, a host of things were troubling me in my day to day life. I knew how different my face was. But I never said a word.

Yet, I would look at other people – 'normal' people. And I would wish that I could be like them. My hatred intensified – for me, for how I was, for having to go to hospital, for the way my immensely-missed sister had been taken from my life.

The more I grew angry and bitter, the more questions raged through my head. Why me? Why I had been treated so unjustly? Why was everyone else ok and happy when I wasn't? Why on why couldn't things have been different?

People often have questions of their own for me. They wonder if I have flashbacks from the car fire. But the answer is no. Sometimes images run through my mind. Maybe they're fragments of partial memories. Or maybe they're just pictures of how I imagined it would have been that day.

The one consistency is that it always scares me. I also had disturbing thoughts of my sister Amanda in the ground in a white coffin. Deep underground. I never ever talked about those thoughts. I couldn't. But the thoughts would go round and round my head merging with my constant conviction that I was ugly.

Melanie before the fire

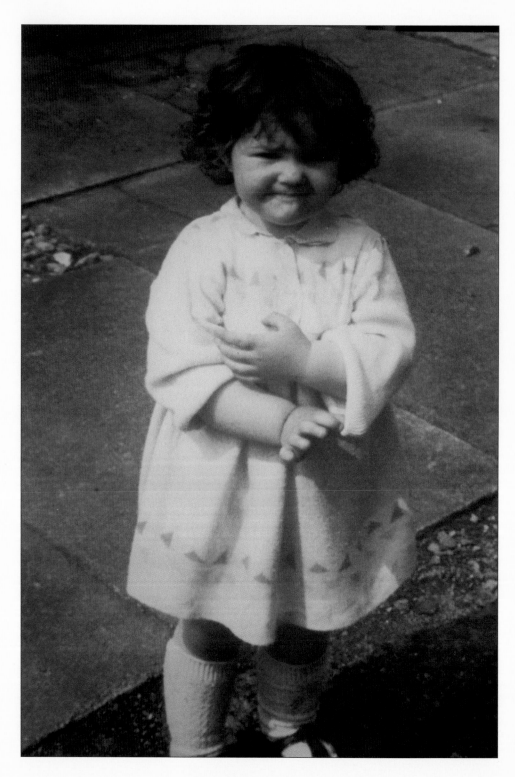

Melanie's sister Amanda

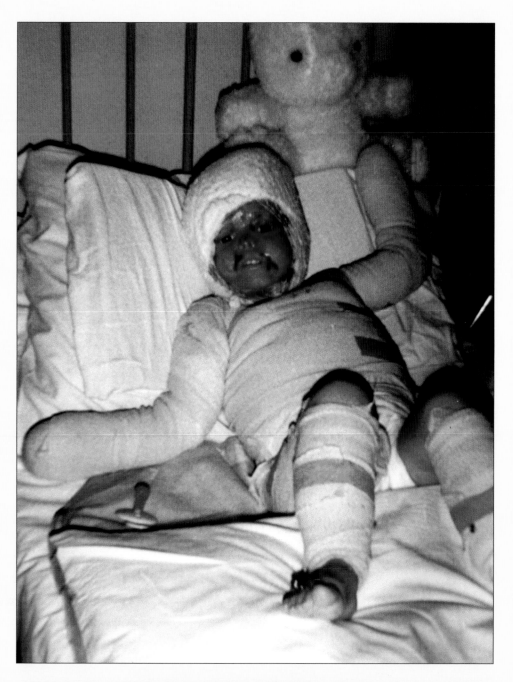

Melanie in hospital in the days after the fire

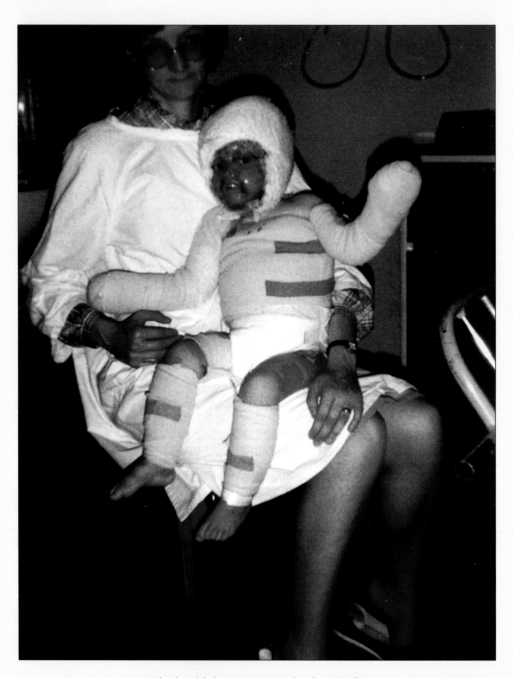

Melanie with her Mum Pamela after the fire

Home again... Melanie and Mum Pamela

Melanie takes her doll for a stroll

Melanie prepares for first day at school

Kidding around... playtime for Melanie

Melanie meets another survivor... Falklands war hero Simon Weston

Melanie takes the reins with the Riding for the Disabled organisation

My parents tried to talk to me. They put on calming music to stop me crying. But it didn't work. There was too much inside me to be held in. So I let it out like an ocean of angry waves crashing against my heart.

One night I wept so much that my parents took me to the doctor. I remember it so clearly because it was dark and I knew I shouldn't have been out of my house in my pyjamas so late at night. We went to the doctor's home as his surgery was shut naturally enough.

I wondered what he could do to make me feel better. But in fact he said that things would get actually get worse as I got older and I started to understand more about my plight.

In that instant I thought to myself: how on earth could it get any worse than this?

I had never had much counselling or psychological help after my accident and the effects of that started to manifest themselves as I moved into the latter phases of my primary school education.

There was also a physical decline. I started to feel unwell on a regular basis. My energy levels were low accompanied by dizziness and fainting. I just didn't have it within me to get up and do anything. My stomach became unsettled and my legs were often painful as if I had walked for miles and miles.

The doctors told me there was no reason for my lethargy and associated problems. There was nothing physically wrong, they insisted.

But even though I felt people were saying I was making it all up, I knew the truth. And the doubters were hurting me.

A specialist in Belfast saw me and all his tests about my physical deterioration came back clear. My parents were told I was going through something akin to a nervous breakdown, caused by everything that I had been through since the fire and bottling up my emotions on the inside.

When I reflect on it all now, I am convinced that my body had just shut down. Everything had piled on top of me and one day something in my head just said that enough was enough and it couldn't take anymore.

As I got older my crying at night stopped. Well, I stopped crying out loud, at any rate. I knew it had been worrying my parents so in order to stop anyone knowing just how upset I was, I started to cry into my pillow instead. I shared my pain with no-one.

But it had to come out. Clearly, slowing down was my body's cry for help. And the physical ailments were its way of unlocking the door to everything I was trying to hide inside. I suppose I knew that it would take a lot of work and a lot of time to ease my depression and to get me back to normal, whatever normal was.

When I was at home, in my own space, I felt more at ease, more secure, more cocooned. I was just me. I didn't have to see anyone or feel out of place.

But at the times I lost the will to keep fighting, it was like a vicious downward spiral.

I don't recall exactly what the medics were saying about me but I do know one phrase they used was "It's in her head"

I now know they meant it was an emotional problem. Back then, I thought they meant I was making it all up.

At school, I realised teachers were becoming concerned with the amount of time I was taking off. One even brought me to the front of the class and implied that I only wanted to stay away because I'd had an argument with a friend.

Nowadays we all know that it's common for people to have days off because of stress or depression. But back then, I was just expected to get on with life, with little or no consideration for what I, as a young child, had gone through and had to cope with.

I was sent off to a psychologist and he explained to my Mum that my breakdown was down to the fact that my coping mechanisms weren't working anymore. I had to find new ones, he said. Which was easier said than done.

I'd never been taught how to channel my emotions and how to safely let my feelings out.

And that is what poor Adrian, my psychologist had to do.

I say poor Adrian because I absolutely hated him. And that was even before I set eyes on him. In the beginning too, I didn't make his job easy for him. I had it in my head that he was trying to prove I wasn't really sick at all. I thought he was just like all the rest of them.

At the start, Adrian was my enemy. But gradually I found myself opening up to him about my innermost thoughts. Talking to him gave my wounds on the inside a chance to start to heal – something which had never happened before.

I realised the process had to start from the inside out. Only by opening the huge glass jar where I kept everything hidden, could the healing really begin.

There really is only so much you can squeeze into the jar before it cracks or the lid doesn't close. And that was just me – the lid wouldn't shut and everything had to come out, one agonising piece at a time.

As my consultations with Adrian developed, they really did start to change how I felt about myself. And I did begin to manage the challenges I faced. What I didn't fully appreciate back in the early days was just how much help Adrian and 'the process' would bring to me in my later years.

BURNING PAIN

No ointment can cool
The burning of
My inner pain.

No stitch can hold together
The pieces of
My broken heart.

No bandage can heal
The cuts to
My bruised and trampled spirit.

No drugs can block
The thoughts in
My hurting mind.

Outwardly I have scars
Inwardly I have raw open wounds.

Chapter 4

Pretty Perfect… Two New Sisters Arrive but I Still Feel like the Ugly One

The arrivals of Elaine and Bethany transformed the lives of Mum and Dad. And mine too. I was just moving on from my childhood and my new sisters helped us all move on in the bigger picture. We had no choice because they were new additions to our lives and they had to be looked after as well as yours truly.

The travelling up and down to Belfast for surgery was draining and throughout my formative years it seemed to be one operation after another. But back in Fermanagh there was a normal family life waiting for us. And I looked forward to coming home to see my new sisters after my sojourns in Belfast.

I enjoyed growing up in a family and loved the company of new siblings and their support. They never questioned how I was. I guess as they were younger than me they never really knew me as any different.

I have to be honest, however and say there were times when it hurt me to watch them as they grew up. They could do things like play the piano and the violin. Yes, I could play them too – but I wasn't really in the same league.

Elaine and Bethany are pretty girls, with lovely hair. And I often wondered what it would be like to be like them. Even for a day.

I resented standing out from them. People would say "There's Elaine and Bethany and there's Melanie, the wee girl from the car fire."

My sisters said to me once that at least people knew my name because everyone would get theirs mixed up. I pointed out though, that people only knew my name because I was 'the ugly one'. Which wasn't necessarily a good thing.

We had a great childhood. We went to the seaside town of Portrush on the Antrim coast every year for a holiday. We played on the beach and we went swimming and horse-riding – in fact, everything we should have done as kids.

Mum and Dad never wrapped me in cotton wool either. If I did wrong, I got told off. Just the same as my sisters. I never grew up thinking I needed special treatment.

I wouldn't have had it any other way because I always wanted to be equal. My sisters never treated me differently either - if I deserved a thump I got one.

I needed that closeness in a loving family environment. Sometimes I did feel isolated but whenever I returned home from life's problems in the outside world I knew I would be safe and secure.

Now we are grown up we are all so different and we do each stand out from one another. We all bring something different to our family and embracing those differences is what makes us sisters.

We live quite far apart now as my sisters are studying at university. We are just like every family in that we have our ups and downs. But we will always have a strong bond. I think our family history helps us all to appreciate that when things get hard, we will always have each other.

As I've said, I have always missed my older sister Amanda. I always felt there was a piece of me missing. Although we were both very young, we still had a bond between us. And that is something which will follow me for the rest of my life.

I often wonder what she would have been like if she had survived the fire.

I sometimes think my life might have been easier with a big sister to look out for me. And I try to imagine what sort of advice she would have given me.

As well as enjoying my family, I also loved integrating into school, just like everyone else. But there was rarely a time when I wasn't bothered by the fact that there was no-one else who looked like me. Yes, I got on well and was accepted by most people around me.

But I knew I wasn't like them. I was the outsider and I pondered on how my day would be if there were 20 people walking round with burns and not just me.

But I knew that I did stand out. And what made me stand out was my exclusivity.

How I wished I could be just another face in the crowd.

I was reminded of that many years later when I bumped into one of my former school-friends during an outing with my son William who was just a few months older than her twin girls.

It was great talking Mummy-talk as we watched our children playing happily in the park.

We smiled together, laughed together and chatted proudly together about our families. But as I walked away my thoughts turned back to our time together in primary school.

I remembered how much I had wanted to be her. She was pretty; she was popular; she was everything I wasn't. I looked up to her. She was perfect. She didn't have to go to hospital. She didn't have people staring at her all the time.

The resentment of being who I was and what I was ate away at me. All the time.

If anyone had told me back in primary school that when I reached the age of 24, I would be like the girl I admired so much and that I would have had everything she had, I simply wouldn't have believed it.

Back then, I just wanted to escape from the life that I knew. Even just for a while.

And that was my dark frame of mind as I went from primary school in Kesh to the next level of education in Enniskillen after passing my 11-plus.

I had been unwell during the latter years in primary school. But even so, I got the results that I needed to enter grammar school.

And it was a new world in more ways than one. Kesh Primary School had been a mixed school. The Collegiate in Enniskillen was girls only.

But it was the old problems which quickly surfaced at the Collegiate. I was told I had to have a classroom assistant. And again I was upset by the move.

The assistant was only supposed to be with me when I needed her – in practical classes like Technology and Home Economics where she would help me with the cooking. They told me it would give me more freedom. But again I was furious at the assumption that I couldn't do things for myself. I didn't want it to become like primary school where I felt that I was always being watched.

At the Collegiate, all the girls of my age – 11 and 12 – were starting to try to assert their independence. And I was just the same.

I was worried enough about going to a new school and making new friends without having a classroom assistant drawing attention to me. However it turned out that my classroom assistant was young, with a bubbly personality and she was a lot of fun.

I got on well with her. And so did the other girls.

My feelings about her softened. All of a sudden, the idea of having a little bit of help didn't seem so awful.

Something else occurred to me in my early days at the Collegiate. For the first time in my life, I realised that I wasn't the only one who was worried about their appearances.

As we got older and became teenagers, I saw that all the girls were focusing more and more on their looks. And they were starting to worry more about what other people thought of their looks – especially boys.

I tried to find out where I fitted into this world. And I longed to look like the rest of the girls. Until something dawned on me – that many of the girls I envied weren't happy with themselves. They didn't think boys would like them and they were concerned with all sorts of things which appeared so minor to me.

But if they thought they needed make-up, what on earth did I need? If boys couldn't accept them as they were and if they felt they had to do something to improve their looks, what hope did I have?

My inner turmoil made me struggle to accept myself. And a lot of people couldn't accept me either. It was clear that some girls simply didn't like me and went out of their way to make their feelings clear to me.

There were others who just couldn't understand how hard it was for me to cope with what I was having to go through every day. Some of them thought it was perfectly acceptable to tell me to get over myself, get over what was wrong.

Yet these were the very same girls who could – and would – complain bitterly about a little adolescent acne.

I know it was difficult for my peer group to understand me. But in a way I couldn't understand them either. I had so much going on in my head that I couldn't really associate with their lives and their trivial 'problems'

In reality, I had probably grown up before my time. I had the worries of an adult which I tried to deal with in the mind of a child. I felt isolated because so many of my colleagues lacked the emotional maturity to empathise with me.

I felt frustrated because I wanted to be like everyone else – anyone but Melanie Grimsley. I was putting on a brave face but inside my heart was breaking. And I wanted people to see through my pretence and see that I wasn't brave little Melanie who caught everything that life threw at her.

Yet no-one really knew the conflicting emotions I was feeling. No-one but me. Yes I kept on fighting because there was no other alternative. But that didn't mean I accepted myself.

And while people probably meant well by trying to cheer me up with comments like "It's what's on the inside that counts" they didn't actually help. Ironically the people who were telling me all this clearly didn't really believe what they preached. In the main, they would be striving for perfection on the outside – with smart clothes and perfectly-applied make-up. Yet they expected me to give up on my outside and feel good about myself inside.

No-one could see what was inside me. Certainly not the girls in my peer group. I wanted to be lovely on the outside, just like everyone else. But few people took the time to think about anything me, apart from my looks.

The staring was one of the worst parts. I knew people were doing it and it ranged from young people to old folk.

I could accept children staring at me because they knew no different. They found it impossible to understand. But I couldn't forgive older people who not only took the time to stare but also threw in a comment or two as well.

One incident in particular stands out in my mind. I was on a bus and two older boys who had just got off laughed at me through the window from the street. They were old enough to know better and I went home feeling really hurt.

It wasn't an isolated incident unfortunately. And all the stares, all the jibes chipped away at my confidence. I tried to be strong but there were times when I just couldn't cope.

After the bus incident, I confided in my diary. My feelings poured out. "I feel beneath everyone" I wrote. "Why do people laugh anyway? It's hardly funny that someone has been hurt in an accident. It makes me feel like a freak show being pointed at and being the centre of peoples' amusement. It makes me feel like I shouldn't be going out"

Well-meaning folk would also say – and they still do – that while it was dreadful what happened to me, I had come out the other side. The implication was that my ordeal was over. But I lived every day with a constant reminder that it wasn't over. That I was still an outsider, an outsider who could never feel the basic human instinct of belonging.

Although I pass certain milestones along the way, I was on and always will be on the same journey that started all those years ago. It's been - and it still is - a hard road to travel.

MASKING TEARS

Back stage things look so different
From the finely tuned performance
You see every day.

When the curtains close and
The stage lights dim,
The darkness hides the real story.

When the hair comes down
And the costume is thrown to one side,
The actress peers out from beneath her mask.

Gladly now she rests behind the curtains,
Happily she would stay here,
Away from the audience.

Without the continued gaze of pressurizing eyes
All with their own expectations
Of what her next scene will be.

Her performance is safe,
Hiding behind her mask
Revealing little of herself.

But now behind the curtain
What has been bottled up is released,
No one is watching, and her tears start to fall.

This is not part of the show.
In the show she is brave,
Confident, an inspiration.

But free from the audience
She is hurt, alone and weak,
Unable to cope.

Her only relief is the closing curtain.
When she can be herself and
Let her feelings out.

But soon the performance must
Start again, the audience are seated,
Expecting their character.

She picks herself up,
Fixes her hair,
Puts on her costume.

She raises her mask
It hides her tears
And provides a smile.

The curtains open,
The audience watch,
The actress performs once more.

I wrote those words in my poem when I was a teenager because that is truly how I felt. By day I was one way and by night another. If I did and said the right things, people thought I was doing well. But beneath it all, behind the mask, the real me felt broken inside.

Chapter 5

Paddling My Own Canoe….but My Joy Turns to Despair over My Transplant Letdown

Life changed for me in 1998 when Mum heard about The Burned Children's Club which was based in Essex.

My aunt Stephanie who lived in England saw it advertised and Mum contacted them. It was a breakthrough for us all because we'd never had any support from any specialist organisation. My parents had just struggled by on their own as best they could.

As the name suggests, the Burned Children's Club supports young people with burns as well as their parents. Every year they hold a camp for the youngsters to attend and when I was 13 I signed up for the first time.

It was an experience which changed my life. Forever.

On arrival at Grafham Water Centre in Cambridge, I looked around the room. It was full of so many people. And I didn't know any of them. Yet I wasn't as uncomfortable there as I normally was in a room full of strangers.

One girl had burns on her arm and upper body. Another boy had burns on his face. Some of the kids looked as if they had suffered their injuries recently. Others like me had burns which were slightly more healed.

It was strange not to stand out from anyone else. And talking about my injuries wasn't difficult either because for the first time it was a two-way conversation. I told other young people how I sustained my burns. And they told me how they got theirs.

If being normal was all about fitting in with the people around you….then at the camp we were all normal.

Mind you, I was still quite shy at camp and I didn't want to sleep in the dormitory with the other girls.

I was embarrassed about taking my wig off but as the week went on my confidence grew. And I found myself talking more and more about what happened to me. No-one forced us to open up but as girls often do, we sat up at night, just chatting. We told our own stories in our own space and in our own time.

During the day, the camp activities included canoeing, climbing, archery and cycling. In days gone by I would have stood apart from everyone else 'in case I got hurt'. But here nothing was beyond the team of volunteers who encouraged, and helped, everyone to participate in everything. And that's just what I did – everything. It was all a far cry from the way I was in my childhood.

Back home people seemed to think that all we did was sit around in circles at the camp, discussing our burns. But we just enjoyed being ourselves. And I revelled in the fact that I was so much a part of the crowd. It was one week in my life that I actually didn't feel burned at all. It just wasn't an issue.

And then there was the relief that no-one was staring at me. No-one looked at me like I was different. Because here I wasn't different.

It made me think that maybe my burns weren't my problem and that part of the blame lay with the society that made me feel like I was an outsider, standing out because I didn't fit in with the majority.

It was other people who stared at me and didn't like my appearance. And it was the media who dictated the rules of beauty and the unobtainable standards which I could never meet.

But in tandem with my changing attitudes to the way society was treating me, I found my own self-belief soaring. In the space of five days at camp I went from a quiet girl who read a book and slept in my own room to someone who was in the middle of everything and having fun.

The Melanie Grimsley who went home from camp was a very different Melanie Grimsley who went there a week earlier. At the end of that week, I realised that what I learnt there and the friends I made would support me through some of the most challenging years which lay ahead of me.

No longer was I prepared to shy away in the shadows. No longer was I on my own. Now, I had new friends – friends who were like me. Now, I reckoned I could do whatever I wanted to do. Now, my burns didn't really have to hold me back.

Just one short week had turned my life around. A week of being a teenage girl hanging out with other teenage girls. Talking about make-up and clothes. And having a laugh.

All the times when I had wished with all my heart to sample an ordinary day in the life of my classmates, had finally become real. But it was even better than I had dared to imagine. For instead of becoming like everyone else and fitting in with them, I found some people who fitted in with me.

Now, only one dream really remained on my wish list. And it was the only thing that the doctors never offered to give me – hair.

The fire left me with only a tiny bit of hair at the back of my head and it goes very curly when it is washed. Just like my sisters' hair. I wrote in my diary at the age of 14: "I look at myself and although I am ugly I love my hair and it changes my looks so much. I have been off school this week and it's been so nice not having to wear my wig. I hate the fact that I have to hide the only beautiful part of myself, the one thing about me that I like."

Having no hair made me feel more different that any of my other scars. Hair is such a feminine thing and even models and pop stars who have their own hair add extensions to give themselves an even more glamorous look.

I'd worn hats as a child but when I went to grammar school, I was convinced that even though they covered my head, my hats drew a lot of attention in my direction.

In my younger days, I had no problems taking off my hat during my playtime but by the time I reached 13, it was totally unacceptable to me. Taking my hat off would have been as private to me as removing my underwear.

However when I was 14, I got news that really lifted my spirits. I was told that I was going to England for a new trial for a hair transplant in a hospital in Essex.

I knew it was only an experimental procedure but it had worked for other people. So I think I just assumed it would work for me. My excitement soared as the plans came together for me to go across the water. I phoned all my friends to tell them when the confirmation of the date arrived.

I could hardly put into words the overwhelming sense of happiness and anticipation. For once my fear of hospital wasn't uppermost in my thoughts. No I actually wanted this operation. I couldn't wait.

In March 2001, Mum and I travelled to Chelmsford and in the hospital they took follicles from her head and transplanted them into mine.

It was only a little operation carried out under a local anaesthetic. But I thought Mum was so brave to undergo all that for me.

She told me she would have given every hair on her head, leaving herself with none. She said it was the best gift she could ever have given me.

The procedure involved removing a square of skin from my head and inserting some artificial skin. That was always going to be risky as my head was the most difficult part of my body to heal. Earlier attempts to graft skin failed and needed to be re-done because the wounds would always break down.

Still, I remained upbeat. I wanted hair more than anything else and I really did believe that the operations were going to succeed. My youthful optimism was pretty unshakeable. But it was a false dawn.

I was out of school a lot during those first few months and by the end of the academic year my grades were starting to fall. I'd always worked hard in and out of class. But the pressure was getting to me – though I would never have admitted it at the time.

I couldn't lay the blame solely at the physical upheaval of the surgery because I was also on an emotional rollercoaster. It was all taking its toll.

At the start of my GCSE year, Mum and my principal Miss Doherty met to discuss what was to be done. They decided it would be best to delay any more treatment for me until the examinations were over.

After Mum broke the news to me, I went into the bathroom and cried. My dreams had collpased around me. All along, I'd expected the procedures to turn out well. I didn't want to put my hopes on hold for the sake of my schooling. The thought of having hair was the only positive which gave me any real optimism for the future. Any normal future.

But the pause in my head grafts turned out to be a blessing in disguise because the grafts stopped healing and the hair didn't grow.

It was a crushing disappointment. And not only did the hair fail to grow but the wound also broke down as before. So I needed a re-graft again in Belfast.

But this time, I was admitted to an adult ward – my first experience away from the children's ward. Talk about a shock. I was only 15 and I still needed a bit of support. In the children's ward, everyone expected me to be scared. Staff explained the situation in a way I could understand. And there were plenty of hugs, plenty of uplifting chats for me if I cried.

But that wasn't the way of the adult world. People forgot I still really wasn't much more than a child. And they gave me strange looks if I cried or showed any emotion.

I think that some hospital staff get too accustomed to seeing surgery and suffering. They forget that they're dealing with peoples' lives. People, like me, who can't go home at the end of the day and switch off from it.

Believe me, it's the most natural thing in the world to be scared of an operation, no matter how much experience you have as a patient. Then there's the recuperation period and the physical after-effects of the surgery. Not to mention how it impacts on your life.

It's all so personal – it's your body; your life, your health. No matter how much reassurance you receive, no medics can guarantee you how an operation will turn out.

When I went to hospital for all my operations, I was basically on my own, away from home and at my most vulnerable. And perhaps strangely, things got worse, not better, as I got older.

As a teenager I got more scared rather than less scared of hospital. As a child there was a blind fear because I didn't know what was happening around. In my teens my fears intensified because I did know.

People were always saying to me that they supposed I was getting used to hospitals and operating theatres. The truth is I never got used to them.

No matter how many times I went into hospital it was always lonely, always frightening, lying there at night wondering how the next day's surgery would go.

Even now, it is still terrifying to think about getting on that table, surrounded by medical staff and placing myself into their hands. In particular, I feared the part where I drifted under the anaesthetic. I could still hear all the voices, echoing around me. But I couldn't see anything except for the lights. As my eyes started to close I always prayed I wouldn't stay in that half-way house between consciousness and unconsciousness.

It always hurt coming round from the anaesthetic as I started to feel the throbbing pain which reminded me of where I was.

Then there was the embarrassment of not being able to wash myself or go to the toilet without help.

In a way hospital took something away from me, eroding my confidence and my independence. Multiply it all by repeated visits over many years and you can appreciate why it wore my down.

Which is why I've decided that unless it is absolutely necessary I will not have any more surgery.

A number of doctors can't understand why I've called a halt. They keep me telling me what they can do for me. But I just wish they could see me for who I am – not something for them to fix.

No matter how many operations I have, or how long I strive for perfection, the surgeons can never make me look how I would have done if I hadn't been burned. I've stopping growing now so I don't need any more surgery to release my skin as used to be the case when I was getting bigger during my childhood.

Anything the doctors could do for me now would be simply for cosmetic reasons. But you know if I started trying to correct everything about how I look, I would never be truly happy. I would probably want this thing or that thing done. And so it would go on. And on.

I would always have the mentality that I'm not right the way I am and that maybe that I need to be altered just a little bit more . I would end up spending the best years of life in hospital and away from my family. Yet at the heels of the hunt, I would still have my burns. And I probably still wouldn't be happy.

There comes a point when you have to look in the mirror and say this is who I am, I can't change it, I can't keep going back, and I've got to move forward.

SILENT TEARS

No one comes to hold my hand
Or wipe my tears when I cry.
Sometimes I think the only reason there are nurses
Is to make sure I don't die.

No little chats or comforting hugs,
No one talks to me about my fears,
The nurses come in and out of my room,
And they don't even notice my tears.

As long as the operation went fine,
And your body is not falling apart,
It doesn't matter how you feel inside,
Or about your broken heart.

It's as if they don't expect things to hurt
Because they just go ahead and do it,
I don't want to say I'm scared or cry,
Because I'll end up feeling stupid.

I have medicine for my physical needs
But no one has cured the pain inside,
I have not been here a single night,
That I haven't broken down and cried.

A medical treatment is important,
But love and comfort mean more,
For when you feel happy inside,
Your body will feel less sore.

(Dec 2002)

WALKING THE SAME ROAD

Ignorance is bliss,
The un-walked path
Has no bumps from where
You have fallen before.

When you know
What lies ahead
You are afraid to walk
And meet it.

Along the way, you pass
The trees you have cried under,
Bridges you couldn't cross,
Streams you fell into.

Walls that tumbled,
Paths that crumbled
Beneath your feet.
You know where it leads.

The well-trodden road
Gets worse each time it's walked,
Marks and scars still there
From the pain and failures of the past.

No map, no shortcut
You walk alone,
Entering the darkness,
Expecting the pain.
You stumble and fall,
Denting the road again.

The failed surgery didn't just leave me disappointed and upset at not getting hair. It also caused me to question my faith – the very faith that had been the bedrock of my upbringing.

My GCSE exams were only months away yet I knew that I was missing vital lessons because of the time I was taking off to get my head re-grafted. I needed my head to heal itself. So I did what I was taught to do for so many years – I prayed.

It was second nature to me to turn to God for help. But this time my prayers came from the bottom of my heart. I prayed to God to heal my head. And I remember that I resolved that I wasn't going to be greedy. Just make my head better, I prayed. I didn't even ask for hair. I just wanted my skin to be fixed.

I didn't think I was really asking for much. We weren't talking about my whole head here. Just a wee square.

In my 15-year-old mind, I reckoned that should have been easy for an all-powerful God. After all, he created us. So a tiny square of skin shouldn't be a big deal, should it?

When I thought of all the huge requests people make to God every day, my little ask about a miniscule bit of skin seemed so small. That is why I was so angry and bitter when things turned out for the worse. How could God be so cruel as to let me continue to suffer when all he had to do was click his fingers and heal me?

Time after time, Sunday after Sunday I was hearing about this wonderful God who loved me. Yet when I really needed his assistance, he didn't bother.

Then I started to think of the bigger picture. After all he'd watched from Heaven as our car burnt in Enniskillen in 1988. And yet he'd done nothing.

God's name angered me. People preaching about his love and compassion angered me. And I didn't want to know about him anymore.

I got fed up with people patting me on the head and telling me "Don't worry. God loves you."

Yeah. That was all well and good when life was treating you okay. But my short life had been anything but okay. I'd endured so much, I'd seen so much and I'd felt so much pain that I just couldn't accept that God loved me.

My disappointment in God ran deep. The Bible was full of promise but nothing took away my pain. All around me I saw Christians praising God for the good times but I knew I wasn't supposed to blame him for my bad times.

I felt that I was, in the eyes of Christianity, wrong for questioning God. I was expected to have faith, to praise God through the good and the bad and to accept that he had a plan for me.

So I kept my anger inside but just as happened in my childhood, it bubbled away under the surface. I still went to church as Mum insisted on it. But my presence in the pews only hardened my opposition to what they were saying. In my view, God didn't care. And that was that.

I never once questioned God's existence. I believed from a very young age that God was there, but what I wanted to know now was why did we suffer? Why did HE let us suffer?

The human capacity for helping other people is boundless. Oliver Quinn had it. He saved my life. Anyone standing there in Enniskillen that day with the capacity to stop the fire would have done so in an instant. So where was God? Where was the all-powerful, all loving God when I needed him most?

They were questions that burnt inside my heart for a long time to come.

One entry in my diary reads "God is the one who has left me like this, he watches me suffer when he could help. I know these thoughts are wrong but they are there, they are how I feel and I cannot deny them. I bet a lot of people do not become Christians because they are made feel guilty about their thoughts so they hide them and never do anything about them. It is a fear of being rebuked that stops me asking questions, so each day I go on wondering the same thing and each day no one answers."

Chapter 6

Boys Will Be Boys…but Will Any Boys Want Me as Their Girl?

No-one's going to pick me, I thought as I sat in that room full of strangers that night. I told myself I shouldn't even be here. My friend and I had gone to an information evening about a local dancing competition a few weeks earlier and I was feeling nervous about being there.

I'd always wanted to learn to dance so I thought I would be brave and give it a go. But as we sat there, the memories of the bad old days at school came flooding back to me – to the days when I was always the last one picked for any team. I wasn't popular and I wasn't exactly in demand. And the only reason I got noticed was for the wrong reasons.

It was the same old story into my teens. By then, of course, the focus had shifted to boys.

It seemed the only way to get a boy was to be attractive. Other girls were soon talking about their boyfriends and about their nights out at the weekend. I had put myself on the shelf before I even let myself think about getting a boyfriend.

I knew I wasn't pretty. And if I couldn't accept myself, how on earth could anyone else?

Even the gorgeous girls around me were having to pull out all the stops to get boys to notice them. So I convinced myself that I simply couldn't compete. I also told myself that one day when everyone's older, someone will be mature enough to see me for who I am. It was a philosophy which stopped me setting myself up for disappointment.

My hopes of finding someone were realised sooner than I ever dreamt possible. And it was partly due to something which we all now take for granted – the mobile phone.

Suddenly, everyone was getting a mobile. And I was no exception - after a lot of nagging at my parents, it has to be said. Eventually however I did get my phone and it was about the size of a brick.

Soon my friends and I were all texting each other and along with the introduction of instant messaging online the era of 'faceless' communication began and it was to work to my advantage.

My friend knew a guy called Brian and she thought it would be a great idea to get him to text me because he didn't have a girlfriend and she knew I struggled to talk to boys.

So I waited that evening – November 21, 2000 - for a message and sure enough up popped a text from this poor boy saying 'I have been told to text you, so how are you?'

I was so excited and immediately texted him back. It was to be the first of many exchanges. We didn't know then just how much profits we were going to make for the phone companies but I was soon texting Brian – Brian Higgins - every day.

I was 14 and Brian was 15. He lived in the opposite end of County Fermanagh from me. His home was in Lisnaskea, about 30 miles away so I knew I wasn't going to bump into him. He went to the boys' grammar school in Enniskillen – Portora Royal – so I knew I wasn't going to see him there either.

His bus went in the opposite direction from mine. So from my point of view it was perfect. For I could chat to a boy and get to know him without any pressure. How I looked wasn't even an issue. Not at the start anyway.

Soon Brian and I were sending each other texts all day, every day and we talked on the phone at least once a week, maybe for half an hour at a time.

We talked about school and what we were doing and how much we would like to meet up. We were braver in our text messages than in our phone calls and we would say how we were enjoying getting to know each other.

Oh yes, you may be wondering about that dance competition. Well, I did get picked – first actually. Once again life had proved me wrong. So I guess we don't always have the answers. And our thoughts about the outcome of any situation can be so wrong.

I have learned to try everything. Otherwise I'll never know what could have been waiting around the corner for me if only I had the courage to take a look. Like Brian Higgins.

It was only after six months of phone calls and text messages that Brian and I actually met face to face. I felt I'd known him for ever and we'd become firm friends over the phone but nerves always stopped us from taking the next step.

I'd told Brian about my burns and I was afraid it would put him off wanting to get to know me better. But that wasn't the case. And I was glad I plucked up the courage to go through with the meeting. For once, I ignored my worries and stopped listening to the doubts going around in my head. And I took a chance.

Brian had told me my burns didn't matter but I found that hard to believe.

We arranged to meet near Enniskillen Castle beside Lough Erne. And our first meeting after school proved me wrong about Brian and his attitude to my burns. For he really did see me for who I was.

I still remember my first words to him. 'Hi how are you?' I asked him as I looked for the first time at the boy whose voice was so familiar to me.

We walked and talked at the edge of the water. And I think we both knew right from the very start there was a definite spark, a definite connection between us.

And it wasn't long before we were meeting up every week to stroll along the sides of the Lough. We would get later buses home from Enniskillen to give us more time with each other. Soon we were holding hands.

We went out on Friday nights, mostly to the cinema but we also found there were plenty of courting spots around Enniskillen!

To my total disbelief I had my very own boyfriend at the age of 15. And as well as all the obvious joys that Brian brought into my life, he built up my confidence no end.

Now, I'm not saying anyone needs a partner to boost their self-belief but at that time I was my own worst critic. Yet Brian totally contradicted my own thoughts about myself and my doubts over my ability to be loved.

Brian constantly challenged my opinions about myself. Most of us will stand in front of a mirror and say we don't like what we see – we're too fat or we don't suit our hairstyle. Few of us can accept a compliment.

That was me all over. I never looked at myself and thought that I was looking pretty. But Brian wouldn't allow me to think like that. It was so good to have someone in my life that made me think about things from a different perspective, a different way round.

And just having Brian as my boyfriend made me feel – for one of the first times in my life – that I was on the same level as everyone else. When the girls talked about their weekend outings with their boyfriends, I could join in the conversation.

I was no longer an observer like I'd been in primary school. And far from being on the shelf as I'd dreaded, I was able to be in the hub of the action, enjoying prom nights and Valentine's Day as opposed to having to listen to other girls' experiences on their dates.

With Brian by my side I didn't feel I had to compete with the other girls when we went out at the weekend. I already had my boyfriend. And so I wasn't concerned any more about what other boys thought of me.

My fears were banished that my later teenage years would be a misery of rejection. And the constancy of our relationship was wonderful too. As other couples got together and broke up, Brian and I stayed together. I was one of only a handful of girls who could say they were going steady.

And Brian really did put the 'friend' into the word boyfriend. I'd prayed all my life for a best friend who would get to know me and get close to me. In primary school, I was always just a little bit detached. Yes, people did talk to me but I was never part of a group of close friends. But now I had a friend who was closer than any other I'd had before. And it was Brian.

But there was more to us than friendship. It was soon obvious that Brian and I had fallen in love. The more time we spent together the more time we wanted to spend together. I realised that love wasn't just knowing I could live WITH Brian – I couldn't live WITHOUT him.

But one of the biggest hurdles lying ahead for me in my relationship with Brian was to let him see me without my hair. I'd no choice but to let him see my face. But my hair was a different story, altogether. My head was always hidden and that was always something of a comfort as it made me feel a little more normal, somehow.

But for Brian to see me without my hair was for him to see the real me. And I'd never let anyone close enough before, simply because I was afraid of rejection.

Brian told me there was nothing I could show him that would change his feelings for me but I wasn't convinced.

Eighteen months passed without me ever revealing that one part of me that I kept so carefully away from his view.

I decided to approach the problem by telling Brian to look at a picture of me without my wig. That was on a website on the internet. The Burned Children's Club had posted the photograph from the camp which had been the one and only place that I felt confident enough to take it off.

I waited anxiously for Brian to text me back after he'd gone online. To see the real me. I shouldn't have worried because his answer was just typical of the real Brian.

I wrote down his reply and copied it into my diary. He said "It was a shock at first but then I saw it was my Melly who I cherish no matter what she looks like. My opinions haven't changed at all. I still love you as much as I did ten minutes ago"

Brian's message summed up our entire relationship. No matter what negative I came up with as to why he mightn't want me, Brian not only had an answer – he had the perfect answer.

Chapter 7

Sad Times, Bad Times as My Grandad Passes Away and My Parents Split Up

Brian made me blissfully happy. But there were other parts of my life which weren't quite so uplifting. Emotionally, I was going through a bad time around the age of 15. I was bitterly disappointed at the failure of my hair transplant trial. I had lost direction in terms of my faith. And at home, things took a turn for the worse.

In December 2001, I'd been in hospital to the skin graft on my head re-done to fix the wound left by the hair trial. I was feeling really low and annoyed that I'd had to drop one of my GCSE subjects.

The pressure of studying was enormous but we had a lovely Christmas that year. The whole family were together including Mum's father Bert Noble – Granddad Bert. But what none of us knew was that it was to be our last Christmas together.

We all enjoyed each other's company over a magical Christmas dinner. But looking back, I wish I'd paid just that little extra bit of attention so that I could remember exactly what we all said and I wish I'd kept all the festive cards we exchanged.

For just eight weeks after that wonderful Christmas, Granddad became ill and he was diagnosed with lung cancer. Mum's life changed dramatically over the next few months as she cared for him. He had to travel to Belvoir Park hospital in Belfast for treatment and the impact of the chemotherapy could clearly be seen in his body.

He'd always been such an active man. He was a sheepdog trainer and he was always out and about. But in just a few short months he was unable to enjoy the outdoor life that he had adored. Yet he never complained. In fact, it was quite the opposite. He didn't want to sit about the house and instead he asked to be taken out to see the places he enjoyed.

Mum and Dad drove him to the wild Donegal countryside and to the ruins of the little house at Pettigo, just over the border from Fermanagh, where he was born.

He didn't spend his final days in hospital, either. He came back to his house and his countryside – the one place he felt truly at home. He died in the July of 2002 and it had all seemed to happen so fast.

For me, Granddad's illness and his subsequent passing were my first encounter with death since Amanda. It hit me harder than I'd anticipated.

During his illness, I withdrew from the situation slightly. I had my studying to do for my GCSEs and that kept me busy. But I really didn't know how to react to everything that was going on around me.

I couldn't understand how someone who knew they were going to die could still find it within themselves to really live and live with such courage. He showed more bravery in his last months than some people display during their whole lives.

Some folk want to quit at the first hurdle but even though he knew his race was almost over, Granddad didn't throw in the towel. No, he kept running to the end.

When he died, it was seeing his coffin which affected me the most. The finality of that coffin.

But as I looked at it, I saw another coffin in my mind's eye – a tiny white coffin which had been laid to rest so many years before.

I used to have dreams about Amanda's coffin in the ground at Sydare cemetery in Fermanagh. It haunted me to the point where I hated going to her grave because I couldn't see past it. My upbringing taught me that Amanda was in heaven but all I could see in front of me was the harsh reality of the ground. Her death troubled me more than I have ever admitted.

Granddad Bert was only 69 when he died. That isn't old but he'd lived a full life and he'd had children and he'd seen his grandchildren. But Amanda was at the opposite end of life. She was only at the beginning of her journey and it didn't seem right that she never got her chance to complete it, to live her life.

As Mum buried her beloved father, she stood strong. It was the natural order of life. But she should never have had to lay her daughter to rest. It was a thought that confused me as our family had to walk again through that valley of the shadow of death 13 years later.

What still seems strange to me in the aftermath of a death is that mourners all look at the body after it has been laid out. I chose not to look at Granddad Bert until the night before the funeral.

I didn't want anyone to see me cry. I'd never seen anyone who had died but Granddad didn't look I'd imagined. He looked so peaceful – unlike the images I'd had in my head when I thought about Amanda.

There was a quiet stillness in the flickering candle light as I looked at Granddad's face. His body was there but the room was empty.

I ran out across the fields that night and stopped at the gate where I'd been with him one afternoon. My parents had bought me a pony called Snowy which Granddad kept on his farm and we spent time out in that field together in the summer evenings.

As I stood there and looked across the fields at the deep red sunset, I knew I hadn't left Granda back in that room - I was now standing where he was. He was there in the beauty of that sunset, in the warm breeze of the summer and he was at peace in the fields of gold.

Although my faith was shaken and I had so many unanswered questions, I knew in my heart that death was not the end. God's beauty is manifested in his creation and as I gazed on the serenity of the hazy sunset I knew my Grandad was with God.

That summer brought up so many questions for me about the meaning of death and about what lies beyond the grave. But most importantly it raised the question of whether or not there can be peace in death? However it wasn't the only dilemma that was to trouble me around that time.

My little world really had been rocked by the death of my Granddad. But shortly afterwards came another major blow as my parents said they were going to split up.

Coming so soon after the death, with all the thoughts of the end of life in my mind, the thought of the end of our family hit us all hard.

As a child, my family was always the one thing I could rely on. No matter what, my parents were always there for me. Without question. Without a doubt. And it was totally inconceivable that our family could ever fall apart. Or so I thought.

But even though I was only 15, I knew all wasn't well between my parents. They didn't argue or anything like that. But there was just a distance which had grown up between them.

At that time, it was difficult for me and my sisters to come to terms with the separation but as I've grown older and can see it through an adult's eyes, I've come to realise that it was the right choice.

For me, my priority was to try to keep everyone happy. Mum was moving into Granddad Bert's house and my sisters were going to live with her. But I thought it might help if I went to stay with Dad - to build a bridge and to make sure he had someone too.

But it didn't really work out. We were all going through a rough time and

Dad was at work in Omagh a lot. So it was suggested that it would be better for me to move into Mum's house as well rather than to be on my own.

I didn't want to let go, however. To me it seemed like giving up. And it was only after a lot of persuasion from both of my parents that I relented and went to live with Mum.

There was be no going back for anyone as Mum and Dad got divorced. But thankfully it wasn't a messy one. And I thank Mum and Dad for that. The children weren't dragged into it and everything was settled amicably between them. Which saved a lot of pain for everyone.

It showed just how strong my parents are. And I honestly don't know how they got through so much – from the death of Amanda to coping with me. It really does take a lot of courage and a lot of honesty to stand up and admit that a relationship isn't working rather than to keep living a lie.

I admire my parents so much for so many things. I owe them an immense debt of gratitude. And when I look at them now, I can see they are really are different people from what they were. And they are happier apart.

Even so, I was glad to see the back of 2002. Christmas Day brought it home to me just how awful the previous 12 months had been. Dad called in that morning and left again to return to Omagh where he now lived.

Mum, the girls and I were in a different house from a year earlier. And Granddad Bert was no longer with us.

What a contrast it all was from that idyllic family Christmas of 2001.

The year had been a steep learning curve for me. Never again would I take for granted everything that I held dear in life. I knew now that so much could change so quickly. In the blink of an eye.

The weight of the world was still on my shoulders as 2003 came along. I was a troubled young woman – an angry young woman who was furious with my entire life.

For any teenager that period between the ages 16 and 18 is an especially challenging one. Growing up is a difficult time. And for me it was doubly hard. Like everyone else I was struggling with my identity but I was completely fed up with who I was.

And like all the other girls of my age, we weren't children anymore, experimenting with a little lip gloss or far too much fake tan. We were young women.

We looked at women's magazines, trying to figure out who and what we were going to become, trying to decide what to do with our lives.

Being at grammar school, we were told we could be anything we wanted to be. All it took, we were assured, was hard work. But I was left to wonder could

I ever be the woman I wanted to be?

As everyone else matured from childhood to adulthood, I stayed the same. Yes, I had Brian and a group of friends who accepted me but I didn't really like me.

I got a beautiful long blonde wig which glistened like gold. It was human hair so I could wash it and straighten it but even my lovely wig would sometimes make me angry because I knew it was fake. Just something for me to hide behind so I could try to fit in.

I didn't really want to go out at all. I just wanted my ugly face and my silly little hands to vanish. I found it nearly impossible to keep up the charade of wearing a smiling mask to hide my tears.

Of course I had perfected the exterior sham so well that people never really thought of what was happening inside. Everyone just expected me to carry on regardless and to do well. And at school I didn't disappoint them. I got grade As across the board. I was top of the class. And it seemed that I could be anything I wanted to be. But I knew I couldn't. I knew that first of all I had to learn to be me.

That summer also saw me having more surgery. But it came at the wrong time. I was feeling really low. And I needed a break from my exams. The last thing I wanted was to be stuck in hospital a week after I'd put down my pen in that examination hall.

And to compound matters, Mr Millar was no longer my surgeon. I had grown up with him but he had retired.

The new surgeon meant well, of course, but he started to annoy me because he wanted me to have more and more operations. Of course, he probably didn't realise how much all the procedures actually hit my confidence rather than building it up.

One of the more bizarre suggestions was for the medics to operate on my nose in a bid to improve the way it looked. The plan was to sew my arm to my nose and leave it there for a fortnight so that the blood vessels could join and knit together before grafting the skin to my face.

The very idea of it was horrendous enough. But I came out of the consultation thinking that my face must be really terrible if he wants to do so much to it.

Personally, I'd been content enough with my nose. But now he'd unsettled me.

He was also persistent about eyebrows. I didn't have any but he said they could take a little hair from the back of my head and use it to create eyebrows.

I'd seen how the procedure turned out on someone else and I thought it really didn't look right as the hairs were too long and too spaced out.

I asked him why he wanted to give me eyebrows when all my friends were waxing theirs off.

That ended the eyebrows conversation.

But I still came away from the hospital feeling down. I'd gone there feeling I was complete and that I was OK as I was. But I left feeling that I needed to be altered, that I needed to be fixed.

Why did people always look at me as something broken? Was it so unimaginable that I could be happy how I was?

And it was around the same time that there was all the hype that I might get a face transplant. No-one actually suggested that I should, would or could have a transplant but that didn't stop the speculation after a ground-breaking operation in France. The word went round that because I had a scarred face that I was in line for a similar operation to the one carried out in France. I was asked to comment on the rumours and one newspaper even ran a story saying that I was going to get a transplant. But it was never a starter. I would never ever have considered it.

The very idea was and still is horrendous. Even having it mentioned made me feel like a freak and there is simply no other way to describe it. Why on earth, I asked myself, would I want a face transplant in the first place? Yes there were scars on my face but they were healed and functioned. I argued that I just couldn't take my face off and put on another one because I didn't like the look of it.

Perhaps if someone was in a bad accident and needed urgent repair work, they might need a transplant which would reduce the necessity for skin grafting. But I didn't like the thought of it myself. And nothing has happened to change my mind.

But even as the face transplant stories were circulating, I was back in hospital in Belfast.

I lay in the bed that June thinking about the good times I should have been enjoying with Brian and my family nearly 100 miles away.

But I was on my own, lonely in the silence and the isolation. The worst thing for me about hospital even as a child had always been the silence and the loneliness.

There was nothing else to do but feel the pain and think about my situation. At that point in my life, I needed a distraction from my thoughts, not the long silent nights in the hospital.

All I could hear were the soft footsteps of the night staff as they checked on their patients during the night. My mind was racing. I was alone with my thoughts. So I wrote a poem.

FEARFUL STORM

The silence is an open window
Letting the thoughts inside,
Offering no protection from
The wind and rain.

They now can come in around me,
The wind tosses me,
The rain slowly gathers
Until I am out of my depth.

I fight with it,
I try to shut it out,
Close all the windows
Before it's too late.

They stay open.
Tossed by the stormy thoughts
Chilled by the wind,
I am no match for the fear they cause.

I am alone, it is dark
I have stayed on top,
But now my tears add to the flood
Of hurt surrounding me.

The storm rages,
I lose control,
My thoughts, they grip me
And pull me under.

Around that time too I was convinced Brian would leave me, even though there was absolutely no reason why I should have thought like that. No matter what poor Brian said to the contrary, I was frightened that he would find someone prettier than me.

Yet again I was seeing everything in my life as negative. It was like wearing sunglasses on the brightest day of summer but still the world looked dark.

I just shut down. Not physically like I'd done at primary school – but rather mentally.

I didn't care about anything. So nothing got in too deep. If I didn't care, I didn't think. And there were times when I barely spoke. Sometimes I gave one word answers to people. But mostly I just shrugged everything off.

In retrospect, I can see I simply wasn't coping. And instead of confronting my issues, I just bottled them away.

At school, too, I was worrying my teachers. And I was also causing distress to my parents.

Every year my needs in the classroom were assessed through what was known as an educational statement which would determine if I required any help.

In sixth form I was deemed old enough to fill in my own assessment form. It made for strange reading. My answers were brief and in my eyes to the point.

Q. Are you getting on well in school?
A. No.
Q. What subjects do you like?
A. None of them.
Q. Do you need additional help?
A. No.
And so it went on. No, no, no.

The headmistress called my Mum and me to a meeting ... a meeting Mum still remembers to this very day.

My form teacher Mr Cathcart who also taught me A-level English was baffled. He said he couldn't understand my responses. In class he said I always appeared to understand the work and I was one of the girls in the class he could rely on to answer a question during discussions.

He was right, of course. I did work hard and I did have a real drive and desire to do well. But somehow, I had just lost the energy to fight.

Now it was a constant and conscious effort to get up every morning and to put on my make up for school. I would rather have stayed at home. To hide.

Sometimes at night I would think about running away. I had this notion of going and sitting under a tree somewhere, anywhere on my own. Not so that I could think about things. Rather so that I could NOT think about things.

I wanted to empty my head and switch off all my thoughts off. A detox for my mind, in a way.

I became almost one dimensional. No-one could reach me, not even Brian.

He told me once that he didn't know me anymore, that I was like a stone.

They were the harshest words he had ever spoken to me. But he was right. It was true – I was still a stone – cold and emotionless. I had locked myself into my own hard little world. And I wasn't sure if I wanted to come out.

ROCK HARD

Maybe you are right,
Maybe I am a stone.
A cold stone
Hardened by life.

A sad expression
Engraved on my face,
Never changes,
Never smiles.

My exterior too solid
To break through to me.
My inside
Has lost all softness.

But that softness
Would bend under pressure,
A smile would shatter
Beneath this pain,

You can't get blood
Out of a stone,
So if I am a stone
I am strong enough
To survive.

THE WALL

How can you knock down the wall of hurt
If bricks keep being added to it?
Each bad experience acts
As a foundation for the next,
And so the wall gets taller.

One brick at a time is manageable,
But sometimes loads come at once,
Piled on top, faster than you can
Deal with the bricks at the bottom,
And so the wall keeps getting taller.

It is too big now to see over it,
Too heavy to move any bricks,
You can't climb over it,
And are unable to smile because
You are surrounded by your hurt.

You sink to the bottom,
Looking up at its height
Which now leaves you in the dark.
Nothing outside the confines
Of the wall matters,
It blocks them from view.

Your failures to get out, add more
Bricks to the top, so you stop trying.
You become its prisoner.
You can't get out.
And no one can get in.

Chapter 8

A Brand New Journey and a Different Direction from the Bus Station Man

The words from my form teacher Mr Cathcart echoed in my mind as I walked down the corridor. I had been the last one to leave his classroom because I was waiting for the class register to leave down to the office.

"Melanie, considering how down you were last year you did really well to get three As in your exams." he said.

My thoughts raced back to that meeting with him, the headmistress and Mum and to the emotional rollercoaster I'd been on for the last 12 months.

I remembered how the people at that meeting who cared about me had been lost for words. While I stared at the table.

But despite it all – despite myself perhaps – I'd performed well in my A-levels in English Literature, Social Care and Religious Education where I'd been top of the class.

Somewhere somehow I'd found the strength within me to succeed. And I think it was at that moment in the Collegiate corridor with Mr Cathcart that the old Grimsley spirit came back to me. I remembered the determination which had carried me through primary school as I strove to prove myself.

Now all these years later the choice was stark – I could either re-discover my old fight and get rid of the negativity or I could wave the white flag and admit defeat.

The time had come for me to make a conscious effort to say that I didn't want to go on feeling low and to remind myself that life held a lot more for me.

I'd built a wall around myself, shutting people out.

But now I told myself that I was going to knock down that wall. Brick by brick. One step at a time.

Shortly afterwards someone else – a higher power - lent me a hand in the demolition.

They do say people find the Lord in the strangest of places. My discovery was in a toilet – or just outside a toilet to be precise – in Enniskillen bus depot!

The re-awakening of my faith had taken a long time. My doubts had haunted me incessantly. And while I was still being brought to church every Sunday, I still wrestled with the big questions to which I couldn't find answers.

Not to put too fine a point on it, I had given up on God. But it transpired that he hadn't given up on me.

Fast forward now to that toilet block in Enniskillen bus depot. I was strolling out minding my own business one afternoon when a man - a perfect stranger – walked up to me and said "God loves you" He wasn't the first person to tell me that but the surroundings were a little bit out of the ordinary.

Obviously I was somewhat concerned. I thought he was going to start preaching at me or at least hand me leaflets. And to be quite honest, I just wasn't in the mood.

I tried to walk on and ignore him. But he stopped me in my tracks. He said "No, God does love you. He wants you to know that. I just felt moved to come over here and tell you that."

I had no idea who the man was. I'd never seen him before in my life. And I've never laid eyes on him since.

All he did was speak to me. And he was gone. No preaching, no trying to convert me. Nothing.

I can't remember if I said anything in reply to the man.

But his words made me think. No-one had been able to reach me because I'd shut them out. But maybe this was God reaching down from heaven to speak to me in a way that no-one else had been able to.

For the first time something had got through to me. And that little ray of sunshine which reached into my heart that day started to warm my soul, melting my frozen emotions.

I wish that man could know what he did for me that day. His words had a profound and powerful impact on my whole life.

He kick-started my thinking in a totally new direction. One which has brought me to where I am today.

Of course, people say – and they say it often – that time is a healer. And although it is a cliché, it also true. The summer of 2003 was definitely a healing time for me.

I enjoyed the break from school which gave me time to relax.

The rawness of my parents' separation was less intense than it had been and my grades in my A levels gave me a real boost.

My final year in the Collegiate was easily my best. My work in class was good and I found myself happy with the learning process. Even when I was feeling down, I would channel all my energy into my studies.

Away from the academic work, I took part in school musicals. Which did my confidence no end of good. I didn't have big parts but as I stood on stage, I loved the buzz of performing. I never got nervous in front of the crowd.

I was appointed assembly prefect in year 14 and I would often write lessons to speak about at the morning gathering.

My public speaking abilities improved with the more and more experience I got. I enjoyed writing down my thoughts to share with other people afterwards.

I didn't know it at the time but it was all a tremendous and solid foundation for talking in public in later life.

By the time I reached my final year in sixth form I had a close group of friends with whom I spent all of my time…. Louise, Genene, Jenna and Jill.

After all the abnormalities of my earlier school life – the time off for my surgery, the loneliness and the hurt - it was good to have a very ordinary and very happy final year.

I was 18 and I had my whole life ahead of me. My band of friends would talk about our plans, our future, our boyfriends and our dreams. And by now I had a clearer understanding of myself and my place in the scheme of things in the world.

I was still talking to Adrian, my psychologist. And he was still helping me to confront my problems, my inner wounds which were more difficult to cure than my physical burns.

He gave me the power to control what happened to me, instead of letting it control me. If I'd stayed depressed like I'd been, I don't know how my life would have turned out. I know I couldn't have survived the mental torment for ever.

There were times when I poured my heart out in my diary. One time I wrote 'I can't wait to see Adrian this week.'

(Mind you, I never told HIM that!)

Adrian never told me what to do but he helped me to think clearly so that I could figure things out for myself and decide where I wanted to go next and what I wanted to do next – and with whom.

Brian and I had to think about what lay ahead for us too. We knew we wanted to stay together. But our lives were pulling us in different directions.

I'd exceeded my own expectations in my A-levels. But Brian didn't attain the grades he had wanted so he had to repeat year 13.

And that meant we wouldn't be able to head off to university as we'd planned.

So I had huge doubts about whether or not I would go to university on my own.

It had always been assumed that I would go on to university because my academic record in school was always good.

I wasn't certain what career path I wanted to follow. But I knew that I wanted to help people. In the end, I decided to apply to do psychology at university because my own sessions with Adrian had been such a massive benefit to me.

But deep down I wasn't sure – even before the grades came out – that I really did want to go to university at all. Sometimes I wondered if I was just going with the flow.

I'd filled out all the application forms for university and my top two choices were Bangor in Wales and Queen's in Belfast.

But another part of me wanted to stay at home to make a home and create a family life with Brian – probably because for so long I'd always thought I wouldn't ever have the chance of normality.

I'd always told myself that no-one would ever want me and that I would never get married or have children.

Another factor which was holding me back from heading off to university was my reluctance at the age of 18 to leave the security of everything and everyone I knew to go somewhere totally new.

It's daunting enough to find myself in situations where people don't know me. But the prospect of having to go home to a flat all by myself with no-one to turn to would have been a mountain for me to climb.

And then there were the uncertainties about what to study. Psychology did interest me. But it wasn't as if it was my heart's desire.

I wasn't one of those people who wanted to be a teacher from an early age and who follow their dreams, their calling through to adulthood. I basically didn't know what I wanted. But I did know that I couldn't leave Brian.

I'd grown up with him in those crucial years of my teens. And I wanted to be with him more than anything else. My life had changed immeasurably for the better since I'd been with him.

He helped me to cope and his love and his support were all important to me. When he looked at me I saw my future in his eyes.

And that is what my heart told me. So I withdrew my application for university.

The decision lifted a lot of pressure from me. My mind was made up and no-one could say anything or do anything now to change it. It was too late.

I knew only too well that I didn't have a clear direction in my life and I didn't know what I was going to do after leaving the Collegiate. But at least I wasn't going to do something that wasn't right for me. My fears about having to move away from Brian and from my family were gone. The relief helped me cope so much better.

All that was left to be done was something I never had any doubt would be done.

And on Tuesday February 24, 2004 Brian did it – he asked me to marry him.

We were out for a drive and ended up at a viewpoint near some windmills on top of a hill. It really was gorgeous and Brian proposed to me in the classic style, falling to one knee and popping the question.

I didn't keep him hanging on for an answer. It doesn't take long to say the word yes.

I was only confirming what every bit of my being had already told me – that I wanted to stay with Brian and to make my home with him. To make my life with him.

Our commitment to each had been sealed. And all our friends and family shared our delight, though there were worried voices warned us that we were too young.

But I knew I had made the right choice.

I left school in 2004 with three A grades in my A-levels, coming top of my class in two subjects.

I left knowing that my teachers and my principal – Miss Kate Doherty – had played an enormous role in my achievements because they believed in me, despite my tendency to let things get on top of me.

However they never allowed me to stop working and ensured that I reached my potential, even if I wanted to or not, at times.

The easiest thing for the staff at the Collegiate to do would have been to lower their goals for me. But they didn't limit their expectations and their support for me made sure that I didn't limit my own ambitions either.

As I walked out of school for the very last time, I held my head high. And I could hear that little voice inside which had earlier whispered to me. "Show them you can do it" it said.

I laughed to myself because I had done it. And I'd done it rather well.

After my 'freedom' from school came the prospect of a new independence. I started learning to drive in that first summer after leaving the Collegiate. But before I could get behind the wheel, I had to have a disability assessment. The instructor told me there was no reason why I couldn't drive an ordinary car, confirming my belief that I wouldn't have a problem. But even so I was so nervous when it came to doing my driving test.

I had failed my theory test three times and so I was eager to do well in the practical.

I knew I had been told I could drive a normal car without any adaptations but I still felt I would be more comfortable in an automatic.

That meant I could keep my hands on the steering wheel at all times without having to change gear.

I drove my little Corsa around Enniskillen on November 5, 2004 just praying that I would stay calm enough to pass the test.

The examiner was quiet all the way round and at the end simply told me that I had passed.

I could hardly contain my excitement. I was overjoyed and Mum who had been waiting for me was delighted too as I drove her home.

She was probably relieved that I would now stop asking her for lifts to take me to see Brian.

The ability to drive myself really was liberating. And the miles weren't long clocking up as I drove back and forward to Lisnaskea to see Brian as often as I liked.

Passing the test had also bolstered my confidence. Not that I really questioned my ability to do anything anymore. Maybe I did as a child but all that was behind me now.

Sometimes, of course, I do get a little bit over-ambitious. Not long ago, I thought I would try to use a strimmer on the garden. But my hands just weren't big enough and I dropped the strimmer, injuring my leg. Not seriously but it hurt for a few days.

As Dad looked at the cuts on my leg he went quiet for a moment or two before saying "Well, full marks for trying."

I knew he would say that because he always taught me to try things and I love him for that. It gave me a belief that I now have in myself. It made me realise that if I believe in me, everyone else will too.

Mind you after that garden incident Dad did also add "If you're going to die trying, it might be better to avoid the strimming the next time!"

During that summer after saying goodbye to school, I said hello to a new phase of my life – working with children in an afterschool club called Active Allsorts in the Arc Health Living Centre in Irvinestown.

I really enjoyed the job, even though it brought with it a few challenges.

The children asked me a lot of questions about me – the obvious questions about me. But I was surprised how quickly they forgot about it again. Once they knew what had happened to me and had their queries answered that was that – that was all they needed to know. Well most of them anyway.

After I told one little boy that I'd been burned when our car went on fire, he looked at me with a very serious face and asked "Well, why didn't you just get out of the car then?"

Another question really caught me off guard after a little girl asked me "Are you a mermaid?"

We'd been doing some art based on the theme of life under the sea. And I just knew the girl was going to ask me something. But I never expected the question about mermaids. She was deadly serious and I reckon it was my long blonde wig which triggered her inquiry. After I told her that I wasn't a mermaid, we just laughed about. And I still do.

Children's honesty and sincerity can be blunt but their attitudes are totally refreshing. But they also have an amazing ability to accept people and it can be humbling to be in their presence.

They could show us adults a thing or two because we can be so slow to alter our mind-set when it comes to someone or something which is unusual.

On one occasion I was dividing play dough between a group of children and one little boy didn't want to touch my hand to take it. His friend rubbed my arm and said "Look, it's just like mine and yours," Re- assured by his friend's words, the little boy's worries vanished and he took the play dough.

The job with the children lasted only for the summer and afterwards I went to work in the local shopping centre, the Erneside in Enniskillen and I soon realised that the reactions of the youngsters towards me were nothing compared to the supposed grown-ups.

On my very first day in the chemist's shop, a woman came up to the till and asked another assistant – not in a whisper - "What happened to her?"

Another woman jumped as I asked her if she needed any help and she said "Oh, my God. I thought you were wearing a mask" Her friends were as mortified as I was.

I don't know if people mean to be rude or if they're just lacking in knowledge. But it really frustrates that they even think they've a right to make any comment at all.

I know I would never go up to anyone and ask them to tell me the worst thing that had ever happened to them. Yet some people assume they have a right to know whatever they want when they see there is something different about me.

Believe it or not, a man once approached me in Tesco when I was doing my grocery shopping and out of the blue asked me if I had been in the Omagh bomb which killed 29 people and unborn twins in August, 1998.

I told him that I wasn't. But astonishingly, he wouldn't take no for an answer.

"Are you sure you weren't?" he asked "You look like you were."

Now whether or not I was in a bomb, I would hardly want to talk about it in the middle of Tesco. But maybe I shouldn't have been surprised as the insensitivity of some people never ceases to amaze me.

My next job, thankfully, took me out of the public eye. I'd only been in the shop on a part-time temporary basis but after that, I went to work in the BT call centre which was one of Enniskillen's biggest employers and where I was just another 'faceless' voice on the end of the telephone.

The only abuse I got there was the odd swear word from a discontented customer who'd been fed up hanging on the line waiting for a chance to complain.

Brian started working in the call centre a few months after me and we got on well, though it wasn't the most exciting job in the world.

But we knew we had to pay for our forthcoming wedding. So that kept us going.

Planning for the wedding was exciting and we couldn't wait for it to come around so that all our wonderful friends and family and work colleagues could help us celebrate.

As the big day approached, there was a lot of media interest in our wedding. Which seemed rather strange to me because to me it was just a wedding. A huge day in our lives but just a wedding all the same.

But as I looked back at all the stories in the papers and on the TV, it suddenly made sense to me why people would be interested in Brian and me. For after the fire and the tragedy of Amanda's death, the wedding was the perfect contrast – an uplifting story where hope had been lost but love had been found. It was, said one journalist, the perfect love story. It was even better experiencing it from the inside!

Chapter 9

Becoming the Wife of Brian as William and Leo Arrive in the Higgins Home

It was like waking up in the middle of a fantasy on that Wednesday morning, August 3, 2005. I could hardly believe that the day I had been planning and anticipating for so long had actually dawned. That the dream was becoming a reality.

Mum was crying when I went into her room, and she said "We've been through so much with you. It's so emotional today." She was right.

Every wedding day is obviously full of emotion. But as the preparations got into full swing for my wedding that morning, I couldn't help think that it was just like a fairy-tale that we hadn't really dared to wish for.

I sat in the hairdresser's getting my new curly wig all put up around my sparkling tiara. I felt beautiful and nothing else mattered.

Like millions of brides' houses, our house in Kesh was just buzzing, a special place. Words can't really describe the excitement as all of us women busied ourselves getting ready from early morning.

The smell of the breakfast was nothing compared to the waft of perfume and the hairspray. And there was enough make-up to paint a small ship.

And amid the fun and laughter, our every move was filmed by Ulster Television. My co-writer Ivan Little was making a documentary about my life and my wedding and he sent a camerawoman Julia McComish to capture the build-up to the nuptials.

Having a woman behind the camera was an inspired idea. Julia was almost as excited as we were. She knew instinctively where she should be. And where she shouldn't be.

With my bouquet of pink and crimson roses and pink lilies, I left the house that morning feeling like a princess. Dad, of course, was there as proud as punch. Just before we got into our wedding limo, he asked me how I was feeling. I replied that I was fine, just fine.

As we set off in the car for Enniskillen, a group of neighbours had gathered to wave us off and Dad told me to make sure that I returned their greetings.

I was feeling on top of the world after a busy and exciting morning of activity. In the car I wondered to Dad how Brian was and he said he was probably even more nervous than me.

But Brian later told me he didn't get out of bed until after ten o'clock and took five minutes to gel his hair. And that basically was that. But it was just Brian … the laidback groom from Lisnaskea.

I certainly wasn't laidback when I arrived at the church in Enniskillen with my Dad. I could feel the butterflies in my stomach as I stepped out of the car, seeing so many people there to greet me. And then there were the TV cameras and the photographers from local and national newspapers.

But walking up the aisle to Brian was the most uplifting and beautiful moment of my life as a harpist played in the background.

Every step I took towards him was a step closer to fulfilling my dream of living my life with him. The Rev Eric Moore was at the top of the church too and that meant the world to me. Eric was our minister at the time of the accident and although he'd moved to a new church in Bangor he came back to marry me and Brian.

Eric had been a huge support for my family and having him there to share in our joy, knowing that he he'd been so close to us all in our grief made my wedding day even more special.

All sorts of worries had gone through my mind about what might go wrong – from getting the ring on Brian's finger to saying my vows without crying. But I needn't have been concerned. It was all perfect.

Brian held my right hand and rubbed my little fingers while Dad held my left hand.

Looking back now, I realise that we were very young – just 19 – but when something is right, it is just right. I've learnt – and I'm still learning – that the best choices you make are the choices you make when you follow your heart.

I may have been only 19 but I knew that I wanted to enter adulthood with Brian by my side.

If ever there was anyone who'd seen past the outside and found the inside it was Brian.

Apart from my family, Brian was the first person who really got to know me. His love and his acceptance healed more wounds than he will ever know.

He was there for me when I got down. And he still is. His love is selfless and his support is constant.

While some other men may desire better-looking women Brian tells me I am beautiful.

Brian had more insight at the age of 15 than some people who are twice and three times that age.

And while he is my rock, Brian is also my greatest challenger. And I know that if I could just believe what he says and act on it, I would be a lot happier about myself.

But my happiness was unconfined on that August day in 2005. And it just kept on getting better.

After the wedding, our reception was held at the fabulous Manor House Hotel at Killadeas, not far from Enniskillen.

The speeches were all memorable as family members and close friends wished us well. I even said a few words myself.

But there was a surprise in store for me. After interviewing my plastic surgeon Dr Roy Millar for the UTV documentary, Ivan Little recorded a special message from him to be played at the reception. Just for me. And the scores of guests.

Dr Millar couldn't be present at the wedding as he was on holiday. But as his message wishing me and Brian well was played on a DVD recorder, a tear started to roll down my cheeks.

So many people have played so many roles to encourage me in my life but it was Roy Millar who totally and literally re-shaped me and my life.

Everything about me that joyous day - from my huge smile and tear-filled eyes to my tiny little finger with its wedding ring still proudly on it - had all been created and fixed by him.

Oliver Quinn, the man who saved my life in the fire, was also at the Manor House and he too made a moving speech.

And as I looked around me in that magnificent function room on that magnificent evening, I could see that I was truly blessed.

My lovely younger sisters looked radiant as they sat at the top table and I knew I'd been fortunate to grow up with them and to grow so close to them.

Dad was the typical proud Father of the Bride and he basked in his moment all day.

Walking into the church on Daddy's arm I realised just how much I loved him. And how much of him I saw in myself.

His determination, fighting spirit and ability to keep going were - and still are – an enormous and crucial part of my life.

As for my Mum, she looked, as always, stunningly beautiful and her pride in me as I left the house a few hours earlier moved me.

Mum had never lowered her expectations for me and therefore I never settled for less either. She has a quiet strength and resilience which has challenged me throughout my life.

As I started my new life with Brian, I hoped that in some way I could be everything to him – and to the children we wanted to have in the future – that Mum had been and always will be to me and my family.

The day after the wedding, Brian and I went to the cemetery where Amanda was buried and I left my wedding bouquet of lilies and roses on her grave. I wanted to bring a little of my life to her.

Amanda would have been my fourth bridesmaid that afternoon and although she wasn't physically with me, I carried her in my heart on my wedding day.

Some people say that a wedding should be the happiest day of your life. And yes, mine was all of that. But the following day at Amanda's grave put everything in perspective.

It was, though, the start of a new beginning.

After a marvellous honeymoon in Tenerife, Mr and Mrs Brian Higgins started our married life in a rented house in the Fermanagh village of Lack where we would stay for 18 months until the completion of our new home in Kesh.

I worked in a few administration jobs before settling into an office with a large timber company.

But I was still unsure of what I wanted to do with my life. However I decided to pursue some further education, graduating from a diploma course in administrative management at the South West College in Enniskillen.

But yet again my life was about to take a dramatic twist – for the better.

One day at work – on the eve of my 21st birthday party – I took awful pains in my lower abdomen and I was rushing to the toilet every 20 minutes or so.

It was diagnosed as a kidney infection but everyone teased me that I might be pregnant.

And when I went to see my doctor that was the very first thing he asked me. Which started me wondering if it would be so bad if I was pregnant. After all I'd always wanted a family.

And within just a couple of months, I was expecting our first child!

It never once crossed my mind that I'd have any problems getting pregnant or having a child. Luckily my burns weren't across my tummy and carrying a baby wasn't going to be a problem.

But I was very sick. However my first scan will live in my memory as long as I live.

Seeing that wonderful picture on the screen and sensing that little heart-beat made me realise that this was a little person. My little person. Kicking and wriggling and so full of life.

However all through the pregnancy, I worried about how the baby would react to me. Would he or she think I looked different?

I knew a little about the science of beauty and I'd heard that symmetry plays a big role in what we see as beautiful. Therefore my fear was that when my baby looked at my asymmetric face, it would be psychologically pro-grammed to see me as ugly.

I dreaded that as the baby got older, he or she would compare me to other people and quickly spot that I was different from everyone else.

My past experience with children had taught me everything I needed to know about perceptions. Children had stared at me before. And some of them were even scared of me – and that broke my heart.

How much worse will it be if my own child is afraid of me, I thought.

I know many people will dismiss my concerns as stupid. But my reasoning was that if other children were scared of me and pointed me out in a crowd... what would make my own child any different?

But obviously there was to be no turning back now. And I went to have my baby in the Erne hospital in Enniskillen where my own life had nearly ended 20 years earlier after the accident.

All my old traumas about hospitals returned as I went to the maternity ward.

It's all so different now but I'm still plagued by the memories of my past visits and I hate the very thought of lying down in a hospital setting.

And because of the damage to my hands, I've always had to have needles and drips put into my feet. As a result, I loathe having my feet touched and getting needles in takes ages because it's so difficult. So when they had to give me a drip to induce my labour all that negativity came back and I froze in fear.

Brian was with me through what was a difficult birth. They gave me pethidine, an analgesic for the pain, but it sent me away with the fairies. I missed a lot of what was said but Brian heard the doctors expressing fears for the baby. I do remember seeing tears in Brian's eyes as in my terror I begged him to help me.

But at 7.52am on Sunday, January 27, 2008 – after I'd been in labour all night – my baby son was born, weighing in at 7lbs 14ozs. After he was handed to me, his huge eyes looked up at me as he lay on my chest. He was so tiny. So helpless. So perfect.

He cried. Brian cried. I cried.

And in that very instant, I realised that I was my baby's Mummy. My son would know my voice, my smell, the sound of my heartbeat. He was part of me and he would look to me for warmth, food, and love.

As I bonded with him over those first magical days, I couldn't imagine how I'd ever thought that my own child wouldn't like me.

Even before the birth, people had their reservations about how I could deal with a baby. My community midwife asked me if I wanted to speak to an occupational therapist about the practical problems.

But that would have been like admitting defeat even before I'd started and my old stubborn fighting spirit was re-kindled. "Thank you but I'll try by myself first" I insisted "If I can't do it then I will ask for help."

Brian didn't share the professionals' doubts about my abilities to look after my own baby.

I was in hospital for four days after the birth because I'd had a few problems with the delivery. But the time in the Erne was well spent.

The staff gave me a few basic lessons in baby care and the most nerve-wracking was bathing my baby. I was worried my little hands just wouldn't be up to the task.

Now, obviously I knew that most babies can really cry in a high-pitched tone in the bath but my baby was screaming his head off.

He was all red and wrinkly and he wriggled as I tried to hold him.

I didn't know if I was doing it right and I was terrified that I was hurting his fragile little body. As a typical first-time parent, I just wanted to get the bath over quickly to stop him squealing at the top of his voice.

The lovely nurse was fantastic, however. She let me wash him and dry him. And she told me afterwards that she would have absolutely no worries about me handling my baby. It was one of the proudest moments of my life.

Not only had I proved my ability to be a Mum to the nurse but more importantly I'd proved it to the person who needed the most convincing – me.

Brian and I named our beautiful boy William, after my Dad. But we called him Will for short – much to Dad's disapproval.

The first few weeks with Will were the biggest culture shock of our lives. We went from having just ourselves to worry about to having a little one who turned our world upside down.

I'd carefully chosen our pram, feeding bottles, and car seat so I knew I could use and open them. I'd practised putting the pram up and down and had picked bottles that I could hold. Nothing about my hands was going to stop me looking after this little boy.

Will's tiny clothes were a little bit difficult but changing any seven-month-old child when they crawl away from you – bare-bummed and laughing - is a challenge to any parent.

I used to get frustrated, though, when I was out and about with Will. People would ask me if I could manage him. They probably meant it in the nicest possible way but it really was the daftest question.

Of course, I could manage him. Wasn't he washed dressed and fed? And he wasn't doing it by himself.

My auntie Myrtle said I should have replied that I couldn't manage at all, that Will had a dirty nappy and ask my questioners if they would change it for me!

Sadly, I was never brave enough to use auntie Myrtle's line. But it made me laugh and sometimes all we can do is to try to see the funny side of things.

And I was smiling again on my 23rd birthday. For I had cause for a double celebration. Because that was the day I discovered I was pregnant again.

Having Will had been anything but child's play and my physical and mental recovery took a long time. But I always knew I wanted Will to have a baby brother or sister.

Brian and I had a few months of disappointment as we tried for another baby.

But then on my birthday came confirmation that I was expecting again. And I was over the moon as I looked at my pregnancy test and it gave me the best birthday present I could have wanted.

Like Will, baby number two arrived on the weekend – at 11.04pm on Saturday, December 12, 2009.

This time I was better prepared for the birth and knew that the new arrival would be a boy.

I'd completed a hypno-birthing course which taught me how to relax and how to be in control of my body and to know what was happening during the labour.

It helped me stay calm and it was a totally different experience.

Despite the contrasts, the two births were the most amazing moments Brian and I have ever shared.

And second time around, I held my new baby in my arms as a more confident Mum because I had no reservations about myself. This time I knew I could do it.

We called our new son who weighed 8lb 5ozs Leo Oliver Higgins.

The middle name was for Oliver Quinn, the man who saved me from the fire.

Without Oliver, I wouldn't be here today. And Will and Leo wouldn't be here either. We owe everything to Oliver and I'm always conscious that he gave me a second chance at life. He is, quite simply, the bravest man I know.

I can't imagine life now without Will and Leo. Everything about them is wonderful, if a little bit exhausting.

I've learnt more from them than from any adult and they've brought me from a nervous 21 year old girl who was afraid of their rejection to a confident woman humbled by their acceptance.

Neither Will nor Leo has ever looked at me strangely and right from the start I've just been myself with them.

I've always removed my hair at bedtime so that they could see both sides of me.

Leo is like so many other children who have a fascination with hair and love to pull it.

He went through a stage of finding it very funny when my hair moved but one day he pulled it too far and he was very upset when my wig came off.

Will loves my hair too and often picks it up to hand it to me in the morning. He enjoys seeing packages arriving in the post with new hair styles for me to try on and he doesn't see it as anything out of the ordinary.

Sometimes I think he'll wonder why every Mummy's hair doesn't come off.

But he knows that I don't go out without my hair. If I start to walk downstairs without it, he'll stop me by saying "Mummy, where's your hair?"

He takes everything in his stride but he has never asked me any questions about what happened to me. Yet I don't think the moment will be too far away.

One day he looked at my hands and said "Mummy your hand is aaow" which in Will's world means it looks sore.

I looked at my hands to see if I had any cuts to which he might be referring but there weren't any so I asked him where he thought was sore.

"All your hands aaow Mummy" he answered. I knew then he was referring to my red little fingers and in a very small way he was noticing their difference. He now often calls them 'Mummy's baby hands' and he even offers to open things for me because he says he is a big boy and my hands are too small.

I rarely object except when he tells me he will get his Daddy to do the opening for me. I will usually find my last bit of strength and do it myself, just to prove to my little son that women don't always need the help of men.

My boys watch me like a hawk and it sometimes surprises me that they copy things I do and have done without noticing even before they came along.

I use my teeth to open lots of things because I can't do it with my hands. Which means that nothing is secure in our house now because Will and Leo use their teeth too. I try to tell them they could probably do it more easily with their fingers. But they just seem to instinctively follow me.

I worry about them as they get older because I don't want them to carry any responsibility for me. I know children can be cruel and I don't want my boys to be picked on in school or asked silly questions about me. I hate the thought of other children laughing at their 'ugly' Mummy.

I know that having to cope with all that is far away. But I just want to protect Will and Leo as much as I can. Will is such a sensitive boy and I don't want him to feel hurt for me. He has always been fiercely protective - even when I was pregnant he would glare at the midwife as she took my blood pressure.

And he still talks about the bad doctor who put a 'sharp' into his baby brother's leg – he was talking about the needle used to immunise Leo.

One thing about my two boys does upset me. And that is the fact that very few people say they look like me.

Now, I know they do look more like their Daddy but there is a part of me in them too. Some people will say the boys look like my Mum or Dad. But never me.

I just wish people would look beyond my face sometimes because the boys are like me in so many, many ways.

And I can't help but wonder if my face was normal, would Will and Leo maybe look slightly more like me than people see now.

I hope I can teach my boys the value of looks especially as they become men. I think that women are so misrepresented to men through the airbrushed images that are thrown at them every day that the true value of a woman can disappear.

But yet in their tender innocence Will and Leo have already taught me an awful lot about appearances. They don't look in the mirror before they leave the house. And if people are nice to them they can be nice back. No matter how the other people look.

The boys have accepted me without ever noticing that I was in some way different. They do what I wish society would do – they can really SEE someone. Not just LOOK at them.

Quite astonishingly, William has developed into an obsessive…about fire engines and other emergency vehicles. He often plays at being a fireman, running around the house, pretending to be on another busy mission with a hose on full blast!

Not only does he see himself as Fireman Sam from the books of the same name but he actually calls me Penny, the female officer in the series of popular stories. It's strange that he thinks of me as a fire-fighter, given everything that I've been through.

Someday he will realise how close a call I had in the car fire in 1988.

I've told my husband Brian it's just as well I am not too sensitive otherwise I'd really struggle with how Will talks about fire.

And as real-life fireman Alan Elliott relates in another part of the book, the Enniskillen fire station played host to a visit in the middle of 2011 by Will and me.

It was strange for me to see the station but I was fine about it until Alan who'd been at the scene of the Cornagrade fire offered to take us for a drive in a fire engine.

I felt my stomach summersault and a shiver ran up my back.

I don't remember the car fire but I do have a sort of sixth sense when it comes to anything associated with it.

Somewhere locked in the back of mind there must be subconscious memories and so every now and then something can trigger a reaction.

We drove around with the blue light flashing and Will, who's normally a very talkative child, was unusually quiet during the drive and indeed the entire visit.

He looked mesmerised and stared at Alan as if he was the real deal, the real Fireman Sam, a hero from a book.

I sat in the back, staring at Alan and knowing that he was a true hero. Like the rest of the fire service.

Chapter 10

The Agony of Amanda's Anniversary and the Guilt Which Just Won't Go Away

We lay outside in our blue tent, gazing at the sunshine through the canvas. Will and I were having a 'tea party' while little Leo was enjoying his afternoon nap. Our chocolate and orange juice were sneaky treats before teatime but it didn't really matter because we were being care free that afternoon.

Will leaned over and said "Me need to tell you something." So I moved my ear towards him because he often likes to whisper little secrets. "You're my princess" he said softly as he smiled up at me.

As I held him close, I felt more than a Princess in his arms. When I am with him and his brother I feel the most beautiful I have ever been.

I don't need to be on the front cover of a magazine. Or for society to accept me. Because I am a princess in the only little eyes that really matter.

Sometimes, of course, I wonder what might have been for me if the fire had never started and hadn't robbed me of my sister Amanda. The anniversary of her passing – April 9 – never gets any easier.

I know some people will argue that you don't need a special day to remember. But it is the one day we can't forget.

I try to keep myself busy. But my mind always wanders back to that fateful day. To where I was. How Mummy felt. How Dad found out. And to the screams and cries that echoed around the hospital corridors as we all arrived in the emergency unit.

I grieve for my sister but to me there were two little girls lost that day, Amanda and me. I look at the picture of myself before the accident and see the carefree eyes smiling back at me, the wispy brown hair and dimpled little cheeks.

That little girl didn't know what lay before her and what path her life would take. And although I'm still here, she is not. All that she could have been was lost that day, her future changed forever.

I know I have to let go. I have to let her die too because only then can I be happy with who I am now. If I look back and want to be the girl with the button nose and the perfectly formed features then I will live trapped in the past forever.

I remember sitting by Amanda's grave once looking up at her headstone, the hazy sunset glistening on the marble. The quiet of spring was in the air that evening and nothing moved only the rabbits playing across the grass. But how I wondered could somewhere so peaceful hold so much pain?

My heart ached as my crying broke the silence of the evening. I talked to Amanda as though she was standing there beside me. And part of me wanted to believe that she was.

I looked at my pink tulips which were laid in memory of all that was and all that will never be.

I kept saying sorry. Sorry I left you and that was all I could think. Did she know I left her there? Did she see me being pulled from the car? Why couldn't I have brought her with me?

I know I was only two years old but I still can't help feeling the guilt. Knowing that I got out. And she didn't.

I try to include Amanda in our events. I remember when Brian gave me a rose for our school formal, I left it up to Amanda the next day so she could be part of it too.

When I was seven, I even made a birthday card for her as well. In my innocence, I wanted to make sure she didn't get left out on her birthday. But Amanda never had a birthday party. She never had her first day at school. She never had a rose for her formal.

She never had the chance to experience the life that I was enjoying and as I said goodbye at the grave that day, I realised that while I'd lost so much in the fire I still had so many important things that really mattered. My heart, my soul and my future.

And I promised Amanda that I would live my life, not just for me but in honour of her too. I told her I would live it for both of us. To the full.

In May 2011, as I reflected on Amanda, I started to wonder what her thoughts might have been and the letter below came into my head as I imagined what she would have said to me. . It's something which I like to read and re-read now and again because I feel deep down it's more than likely exactly what she would have told me as the big sister I never got to know.

Dear Melanie,

I want you to know that I never left your side once I saw you get out of the car. I knew it was alright for me to go.

You see I am not as strong as you, my injuries would have been too much for me and I too saw a hand reach in for me. You took Oliver's and I took God's.

You are the oldest now and you must do a few things for me, little sister.

Firstly look after Mum and Dad because they are going to miss me. It takes a lot of courage for them to fight for you Mel, they have to be strong when you are not and carry you until you are able to stand.

Every time you miss me I want you to remember that we are only parted for a short time and I will see you again. You must treasure your memories and make them last because I want to hear all about it when we meet again.

I have lost my life but you have been given yours a second time round. Live it for us both, do everything we would have done and bring a little bit of it to me sometimes.

Never forget me but don't let the memories keep you in the past.

You have a future and life can flow through you. Don't let my death become the death of everything you can live for.

I will always be your big sister and I will watch over you until I can be with you again.

Love You All

Amanda

But Amanda wasn't the only person I missed from my life. The man at the Enniskillen bus depot had made me think. He helped me dismantle the barrier which had kept someone else special out of my life.

I was now enjoying a normal lifestyle which not so long ago I feared was not going to come my way. But as I progressed more and more in my life I started to think more and more about everything to do with my life.

The message from God which the bus depot man delivered to me made me open my mind and open my heart to the thought that God still loved me.

And with the barricade down, I was able to see things more clearly and it made me less determined to see the worst in everything.

Still however I kept thinking about why God had let Amanda die.

I'd always viewed it that God allowed her to die and took her from us. He wasn't there for us as we were trapped that day. But what if Amanda's death was evidence that God WAS there?

Sometime earlier, I'd had a long talk with Dad about Amanda. It was back in March 2005 and I told him how her death disturbed me. He told me how it had haunted him too but he said that that one night a man who was a minister came to the door.

The caller said he'd come with a verse from the scriptures for Dad. He said he felt compelled to pass it on, even though he said he didn't know exactly why the verse would be important to Dad.

My father knew right away.

The last part of Isaiah 57 verse 1 says "….the righteous are taken away to be spared from evil."

The passage spoke to my father with more power, he said, than any human word could muster. That verse told my Dad, direct from God, that Amanda was taken to heaven to escape a life of pain.

When Dad told me that, it suddenly dawned on me that in wishing that my sister had lived I was wishing her a life like mine. A life of hospitals, pain and psychological distress.

Amanda was in the fire longer than me and none of us know how she would have been if she'd got out. She might have had far worse problems than me. She might have lost her limbs, her sight and her hearing. And the carbon monoxide might even have left her with permanent brain damage.

She might have had to watch me re-claim my independence and press forward with my life while her own injuries could have robbed her of any future worth having.

She was also older than me and who knows what mental torment she might have faced as she remembered the horrors of the fire. It's all conjecture, of course, but one thing is for sure – her life wouldn't have been easy.

Yes, of course I still wanted Amanda to be alive but not in a life of suffering. For all those years, I'd only been concerned with my loss in losing her. But what about what she would have lost if she'd come out of that fire. It might have been a loss which was too great for her to bear. And so it became clear to me that God in His mercy lifted her that day in His loving arms and took her home. In death she was saved.

I prayed that night like I had never prayed before. I asked God to give me peace. And in the words of the beautiful hymn "It is Well with My Soul" that night peace like a river attended my way.

All my bitterness and anger over Amanda's death melted away and I saw the beauty of Heaven for the first time since her death. Dad told me to stop thinking about Amanda in her grave, to take her out of the ground and to imagine her somewhere else.

Soon afterwards, I bought an ornament of a beautiful angel. She has long flowing dark hair and she's called "Star of Heaven"

And she is now my focus whenever I miss Amanda. I believe that as any older sister does, she has gone ahead of me and is waiting to show me the way.

No-one can honestly know what Heaven is like – it is the one thing which God has hidden from us. But I believe that Amanda is there and that she can see us and watches over us.

When I held my boys for the first time I hope Amanda knew the joy of those little lives which have sprung up from our tragedy.

I also hope that in my lowest lows she asks God to let me feel His presence and that in feeling God's touch maybe I get a little bit of hers too. Although she's in Heaven, I'm convinced part of her lives on in me because every time I feel like quitting, there's something that stops me hitting rock bottom. And I think it's Amanda who ensures that I can't give up.

She never lets me forget the gift of life and that's one thing we can all so quickly forget in the midst of the trials we face. Her death reminds me that I have life – one which I nearly lost.

It's not easy for me to say – and it's taken me years to even allow myself to think this way – but for the first time I'm seeing God in my situation rather than outside it. After Dad had told me about the verse in Isaiah 57, I went on to read the full chapter and it says "...the righteous are taken away to be spared from evil. Those who walk uprightly enter into peace; they find rest as they lie in death." (NIV).

Believing that Amanda is at peace has allowed me to find some peace too.

I wish with all my heart that Amanda and I could have had the opportunity to see what life held for us. But considering the options I'm glad that she didn't have to suffer.

She fell asleep on earth and woke up on the edge of a rainbow. In the arms of Jesus.

ANGEL'S WINGS

I used to think it had engulfed you,
In some way defeated you, stole you away,
But maybe this is not the case,
Maybe you just chose not to stay.

You spread your wings
And rose up high, leaving this pain behind.
You didn't let it grasp and destroy
Your body and your mind

You now are free, you fly ahead
Your name is among the stars,
And even though I miss you
I am glad you escaped these scars.

My own wish is that someday,
I can be like you,
Stop letting it defeat me
And rise from these ashes too.

Chapter 11

Counting My Blessings and How My Wigs Helped Put Me on Top of the World

No sooner had I answered the question that had tormented about Amanda's death than another one followed right behind. My logic in finally accepting that God had saved my sister by taking her to Him opened up another inevitable concern for me. And that was why had God left me alone to suffer?

But after I prayed for peace that night in Dad's house, the rawness of my pain gently eased. And the sharpness of my heart started to soften. I closed my eyes and instead of seeing our car burning and God above us watching, I saw his hands coming from Heaven to carry Amanda to Him.

It wasn't my time to go to Him so He sent other hands to save me. They belonged to Oliver Quinn, an extraordinary man whom God knew would be courageous enough to help me.

I know some people will say it was just coincidence that Oliver was walking past the car. But I'm convinced it was too perfect to have happened by chance.

We live in a world where bad things occur, not because God wants to but because our world, our lives have been allowed to operate according to our free will.

God's world was perfect when he made it but people turned away from God and imperfection entered as a result.

For years, I could only see our tragedy. I'd always asked why me? But after realising that bad things are commonplace, it was a case of why anyone?

The Bible describes God as God the Father, and like a Father he often has to watch as his children make their own mistakes. Just as our own children sometimes have to learn the hard way.

Take my son William for example. One day he wanted to go out in a downpour because he just loves the rain. I knew he'd get soaked and it was also a particularly cold day. But there was no stopping him. So I prepared him the best I could in his coat and wellies. And off he went.

I got a hot water bottle ready and a towel and shortly afterwards he was back – crying. He pulled his wet clothes off and sobbed that he was cold so I wrapped him in the towel and gave him his hot water bottle with its Thomas the Tank Engine cover.

I had known it would end in tears but I let him go out to find out for himself.

But I believe that God cannot wrap us in cotton wool, sheltered from all harm, living like robots. He watches our lives and knows when our plans won't turn out right or go beyond our control. But God can't stop the course of our lives. Instead, I'm convinced that He puts things in place to help us along the way. Just as I did on that rainy day for Will.

But could he have saved me? Yes, he could. But then he could have saved His own Son. But he didn't. He allowed Jesus to die on the cross.

Through that sacrifice by Jesus, I have a hope of Heaven. And that goes beyond anything that happens on earth. God, in his love for us, didn't spare his own Son from suffering and that thought made me feel ashamed that I'd often demanded from God that he should have clicked his fingers and saved me.

Of course, another argument in the context of the world's suffering is why God should have saved me while so many millions are suffering and dying every day.

I was not saved from going through the fire, but I was carried out, and lifted up.

Instead of an almighty God on his throne watching us all go through our lives without a thought for us, I realised that God had compassion on us.

Some people teach about how sin entered the world and so we live in a place where bad things happen. Yes, it's true that we do live in an imperfect world. But we should never – as I did – lose sight of how much God loves us.

He didn't just say "Oh well, it's a fallen world, you brought it on yourselves, so get on with it."

He came to earth to meet us, to join with us in our suffering so that in becoming like us, we can one day become like Him.

There is, of course, no theological or logical debate that can ever give us definitive answers. We have to believe that in as much as God is our powerful ruler He is also our Father who loves us beyond our own comprehension. We have to trust that His decision is right because He knows best.

I asked a well-known theologian once where God was while our car was burning. I still had this image of God looking down and abandoning me. The theologian gave me a very educated and worthy answer straight from a text book. But it didn't relate to me at all. He answered as if God was a distant God with no connection to our feelings and no understanding of our emotions.

So where do I now believe God was when the car went on fire? I think He was right beside me.

God knew I was going to fall, and he had his arms open, ready to catch me.

I stopped feeling guilty over my anger at God. I saw from reading the Bible that I wasn't the first person who felt doubt, fear and even anger.

My favourite verse when I was 17 was in Psalm 69 where King David says "Save me, Oh Lord, for the waters have come up to my neck...I am worn out from calling for my God."

Even Jesus, God's own Son, asked for his cup of suffering to be removed from him if it were God's will. We are not pre-programmed with the ideal responses to our situations. I believe that God gave us our own minds in all their complexity, a vast depth of emotion and a heart with longing for love. Therefore he expects us to hurt, and cry and question. It's who we are.

I needed that time in my life to question, to grieve for what I lost and to be angry at what happened. It was too much hurt to keep inside and in letting all that infection out, I allowed the wound to start to heal.

And heal it did.

At the same time I decided to edit two little words out of my vocabulary – 'What if?'

Small words but they were a big part of my growing up. Throughout my childhood I used them again and again. What if this hadn't happened? What if my life had been different?

But now it was time to get rid of them completely. There was no time machine to take me back to make it all better. I knew that sticking in the past was stopping me from moving on.

Yes, certainly I didn't like how I looked and I wanted to change. I wanted to look like I would have looked if there had been no fire and I couldn't accept how I was now. I didn't really see my face as my own.

I used to dream of waking up one morning looking normal. I would have welcomed people staring at me for the opposite reasons they stare at me now. Oh, how I longed to know how it felt to be beautiful.

But Dad had laid it on the line to me. "You have two choices in life" he would say "You can lie down and give in to it. Or you can get up and fight"

He was right. I couldn't do an awful lot about most things which had been taken out of my hands. But this was different – I did have it in my own power to put up a fight.

Mum would always say too that I needed to focus on what I could change rather than to focus on the things I couldn't alter.

Once I reconciled myself to the fact that the car fire had happened and couldn't have been prevented, I stared to accept my fate. And my face.

I remember saying to myself "Right, this is how I am. No amount of surgery can make me what I could have been. No amount of wishing will turn the clock back.

Now, don't get me wrong. I'm not saying I would choose to look like I do and obviously I would prefer if I didn't have my burns. But while I'm not happy, I now have a freedom, a contentment that means I don't spend my life wishing my face away any more.

Some folk think that people with a facial disfigurement don't care about how they look. But not me. I make a lot of effort with my make-up and my hair. I try to wear smart clothes and I love dressing up for special occasions. I may look different but that doesn't mean I can't look nice.

Some people reckon that fake tan and hair extensions are just for the beautiful people. But why can't I make the most of what I have? At the end of the day, isn't that just what everyone is doing?

We all add a little bit here and a little bit there to accentuate our natural assets. And besides it would be wrong if people were trapped in a world where they couldn't leave the house to buy a newspaper.

For me one of my most vital accessories is my wig. I need it to help me fit in and I know now that I'll never have my own hair but at least I tried with the transplants experiment.

My head is like any other private part of my body. I would never go out with my head uncovered. It's the one part of my burns which I can actually hide and it's good that I have that option.

I can put on a wig and blend in with everyone else. It's not denying who I am now - it's just remembering who I was before. Hair is such a feminine thing and I am such a 'girly girl', I just couldn't imagine my life without it.

It gives me confidence and when I look around at the glamorous world of celebrities and models, I see that none of them go out without their hair extensions, their plastic surgery and their make-up. So why should I?

I got most of my wigs from Therese Hughes who runs Tresses hair boutique in Newry. I've known her since I was 12 and she's gone from supplying wigs to a nervous pre-teen to styling for a beauty-conscious young woman. She did so much for me down the years in making me feel normal, fashionable and pretty.

Any resentment I had about wearing a wig evaporated after I spent time with her because she made something glamorous out of something which embarrassed me.

Her dedicated wig store has private cubicles where customers can try on hairpieces from a huge range of the latest styles. There is always something to suit everyone.

I used to look forward to my visits to her in my teenage years because the wigs were the only part of my appearance over which I had control.

Nowadays, I don't just want to feel okay about myself. I want to feel great.

I decided long ago that I wanted to stop comparing myself to everyone else and to create my own image. And while other people stared, the worst comments about my appearance came from me. I wanted to discover things about myself that I could like.

I believe we need to stop letting other people dictate to us and define beauty for ourselves. And we shouldn't only feel beautiful if we're wearing the season's latest fashions. Instead it should come from who or what we are.

As I got older my scars weren't always the first parts of me I saw in the mirror. I started to think to myself that my make-up was looking good or my new hair colour suited me.

It may sound strange but the more I started to look positively at myself the more other people seemed to give me a compliment.

I went for a facial the other day and the beautician said to me that my skin was so soft. In the old days I would have thought that it was scarred and ugly but I could see now that my skin WAS soft. Probably because I've spent my entire life moisturising it.

In April 2011, as I watched the Royal Wedding on television, I thought that Kate Middleton was one of the most beautiful women I'd ever seen. My old childhood envy returned and I wished I could know how it felt to be like her. To have people stare and say "Oh, she's gorgeous" rather than to have them whisper "Funny face" as they did with me.

But the contrast is that I now believe I can be beautiful. Maybe not like the Duchess of Cambridge – but in my own way.

And someday people might just stare at me not because I'm ugly but because they know me and they like who I am. Just as I do.

Chapter 12

Changing Faces and How I Started to Give a Helping Hand

The happiness I've found in my family life as I've grown older has been reflected by the happiness I've discovered in my working life.

I'm a secretary for the Presbyterian Church in Enniskillen and I'm there three mornings a week. Not only is it the happiest I've ever been in the workplace but the part-time nature of it gives me more time to spend with Will and Leo.

I love what I do and the brilliant people I work with – and I now count them as friends as well as colleagues.

I treasure the time the job gives me to be just a Mum and although it's by far the most challenging role I've ever had, the rewards come back tenfold. There is something so satisfying about just enjoying life. I'm not rushing about or waiting for the next big thing. I'm just taking the time to enjoy, to appreciate what I have now.

Something else has come along to give me another fresh sense of purpose and direction – telling people about my story.

A few years ago I was invited to speak at a meeting in Colaghty Parish Church near Lack in Fermanagh. I talked a little about my faith and my life and I found that I enjoyed the experience of sharing with the women in the group.

Now before you say it, I'll admit that we women do like to talk and before I knew it word was out and I was soon getting calls from other church groups around Fermanagh to visit them.

I also became involved with a charity called the Northern Ireland Changing Faces group.

The charity started off in England and has its headquarters in London. I used to get newsletters from them when I was a child and I often wished that their self-esteem workshops and counselling services had been available to me here in Northern Ireland.

So I was delighted to see the formation of a branch in Belfast and I was only too pleased to play my part. I now raise funds for them and during my talks to the various groups, I speak about the role of Changing Faces.

I fervently hope that more help can be provided for families affected by facial disfigurement here because psychological support is crucial to everyone's healing and quality of life.

I love doing my talks. I never really knew what I wanted to do as a child but I did always say I wanted to help people.

When I stand up to speak I just hope that I can in some small way help my listeners even if it's only to say that I can understand some of what they're feeling.

As for my surgery, I don't need to go to hospital at the moment. But it will probably become necessary for me to return in the future if and when my skin tightens.

I also worry about my hands and what will happen as I grow older. In the sub-zero temperatures of the past few winters, my fingers have become extremely painful.

And I sometimes wonder what age I will be when I need help to get dressed.

Maybe I'll also have to stop driving and perhaps I'll get arthritis and lose the movement in my hands.

But none of us know what the future holds. And with the right care, I will hopefully hold on to the one thing I've always fought for – my independence.

&)CR

The waves washed up onto the sand and the sun shone as we lay on the beach. Leo was on my knee, his smiling face was once again looking up at me. Will was wrecking my sandcastle again, laughing as he asked me to build yet another one for him to destroy. I looked up at the blue sky and for the first time I slowly realised, I was truly happy.

People had told me my life was what I made it. And I'd made it good. I thought about what I had and the people in my life and I could see I'd been given so much.

I stopped focusing on how UNLUCKY I was to have been in such a freakish accident on April 9 1998 but instead to concentrate on how LUCKY I've been in so many amazing ways:

*How fortunate I was in having Oliver Quinn on the scene of the fire.

*What a blessing it was that the accident happened only a few minutes away from the Erne Hospital.

*All my initial treatments went well.

*I had the use of all my limbs and my senses.

*My mental ability was unimpaired.

Suddenly I stopped seeing myself as a victim. But rather as a survivor – a little two-year-old survivor who'd fought her way through the flames to cling on to her life. I didn't lie down and die back then. I certainly wasn't going to do it now.

From the medical perspective, I saw as I looked back through my childhood years and the hundreds of operations I went through that it was miraculous that I had no major complications during any of them.

They tell you that every anaesthetic you have carries a risk. But my surgery was successful and as well as that my development as a child wasn't hindered by it. I excelled in school and with a little help I healed on the inside as well as the outside.

I also had my parents to pick me up, to encourage me, love me and fight for me.

If they had fallen at the first hurdle, I have no idea where my family would be today.

Mum and Dad have undoubtedly shaped me into who I am, right from their first defiant words that they wouldn't hide me away. They instilled in me the pride that didn't let me be ashamed of who I was and they taught me I could have the life I wanted no matter what problems presented themselves along the way.

Mum recently said to me that she never worries about me. I have a job, a husband, my children and I'm happy - with a good education behind me. "What more could anyone want for their child?" she asked "Except maybe for an easier path to get here."

I slowly saw my life not as a defeat but as a victory over what could have crushed me.

In writing this book I've gone over all the details of the past - from the ashes of the fire to where I am now. And when I look at all that's before me and where I have come from, I can now truly say that I am happy.

To wish the fire hadn't happened is to wish myself away and to deny who I am. That accident has not only marked me physically but it has shaped the very essence of the woman I am today. This is who I am meant to be. This is the road I walk. And I'll keep walking.

But I thank God I don't walk it alone. And I never have.

No man is an island, they say. And no woman can stand alone either. Yes, there've been times when I've felt alone and cried alone and wanted to be left alone. But the truth is that for every step along the path, there've been people around me to help me along the way.

I don't tell my story as if everything in it has been down to me. For without the help of so many people in my life, I wouldn't even have a story to tell.

And I know that as I walk forward from this point on, I have my family behind me; God in front of me; and my beautiful husband and boys beside me – holding my hands. Waiting for the next chapter.

Part Two

By Ivan Little

Chapter 13

The Mother's Story… My Tears and Fears and the Shop I Will Never Visit Again

At least once a week Pamela Grimsley has to drive along the Cornagrade Road in Enniskillen past that place. Past the very spot where the shocking fire killed her beloved daughter Amanda and blighted the life of her precious second born child Melanie.

But Pam never stops her car or returns to the store that she last visited in April 1988 to buy a pint of milk.

"My mind goes back to it, of course. " says Pam "It is something I have to live with. But I have no intention of ever going into that shop again."

Like so many other people who think back to that fateful day, Pam remembers the unusually warm weather. "Yes, Spring was definitely in the air" she says. "The week before was great too, we got out and about a wee bit."

That Saturday started off as normal with no inkling, no foreboding for Pam that a tragedy was lurking around the corner.

It had been a happy week for the former Pam Noble whose sister Stephanie was home in Fermanagh from Birmingham to visit her relatives.

Pam says "There was nothing to suggest that this was going to be a life-changing day for me and my family. I picked my sister Stephanie from my parents' house and Amanda and Melanie were with me. We went into Enniskillen and spent some time looking around the shops.

"I can remember sitting in the Diamond eating ice-cream before I left Stephanie to the bus depot and headed home."

On the way back to Kesh, Pam realised that she needed milk. So she stopped at Rooney's shop on the Cornagrade Road. She was expecting to be away from the Maestro car and her two children inside for no more than a couple of minutes.

But inside the store, Pam heard someone shouting that a car was on fire. She says "My heart sank. I had an awful feeling it was my car. When I ran out of the shop the Maestro was on fire and there was lots of smoke and flames.

"Melanie was being rolled on grass after a man I now know to be Oliver Quinn had rescued her. I ran over to the car to see if I could get Amanda out. I was shouting that there was another child in the car. But the heat was terrible. It's so hard to put my feelings into words but I couldn't quite understand what my eyes were seeing.

"There are some things in life that defy words and that was one of them. But I felt that God was with me. I felt that He was standing at my shoulder.

" Melanie was handed over to me. She was screaming. Her two wee hands were held over her face and they were burnt so badly."

Pam was grateful that the Erne Hospital was close by, just a few hundred yards away in fact. A man who was on the scene told her he would bring her and Melanie there. She has no idea who he was but he brought her to the Erne and she thinks he was driving a van.

Even amid the panic and pandemonium in the seconds after coming out of the shop, Pam had no doubts about the extent of the nightmare facing her and her girls.

"When I saw Melanie, I was pretty sure I would never see Amanda this side of eternity again."

At the Erne hospital, a policeman came to see Pam. He had tears in his eyes. Pam didn't need him to say a word. She knew what he was going to tell her – that Amanda had perished in the fire.

At the hospital, Pam was joined by her sister Stephanie who'd been on her way to Belfast on a bus, the first stage of her journey back home to England.

"The police went after the bus and brought her back to Enniskillen but she didn't know why" says Pam whose husband William soon came to the hospital along with her Mum and Dad.

They were all told the devastating news that Amanda was gone, that Melanie was critically ill and that doctors didn't know if she would live.

The Grimsleys didn't go straight home from the hospital. Instead they went to a friend's house to get what Pam says was "a wee bit of space"

However on the road back to Kesh, Pam says it dawned on her that she had not only one funeral to prepare for but possibly two. "We simply didn't know if Melanie was going to survive".

Back at Kesh, a doctor came to see Pam and left her Valium tablets. "He looked at me and said 'it hasn't hit you yet.' But I think it had.

"Our minister the Rev Eric Moore came and lit the fire for us and just held us. Sometimes there are no words. And when there are no words it's wise not to say anything at all. A touch conveys a lot in times like that.

"A relative of William's came with a big box of groceries and I thought how kind - we won't have to go to the shop for a while. I didn't realise that there would be a wake and the groceries were for that. I had no idea that so many people would be coming to the house.

"I found that hard because of my grief and because I'm a fairly reserved person and I find speaking to lots of people difficult. I cried myself to sleep that night, unable to understand how I was going to get through the next few days. My Dad stayed with us, sleeping on the sofa."

The next morning Bert Noble brought the family to Belfast to see Melanie. "I remember just breaking down in tears every few minutes. "says Pam.

Amanda's funeral was huge. "It touched me deeply that so many people came. There was a real sense of grief in the air and I felt that people were genuinely sharing in my pain. I received lots of cards and letters too which helped me. God's presence was very real to me in those hours and days. He doesn't leave us when we need Him.

"I have always felt that God's heart breaks when He sees His children in pain, just like any father's heart would. I relied heavily on the prayers of other people in those early days because I was not able to pray for myself. I felt upheld and strengthened. "

Pam says she gets annoyed when she hears people blaming God for tragedies.

"Death comes from man, not God. I believe that Amanda is with God. One day I shall be there too so that keeps me going. Christians don't mourn like those who have no hope. My life span on this earth is very short compared to all eternity, so I shall be longer in Heaven than on this earth.

"But I thank God that He is able to heal the broken hearted and pour His love upon us here on earth. The Psalmist said 'I would have fainted unless I had seen the goodness of the Lord in the land of the living.' God takes the broken pieces of our lives and helps us build them up again if we will allow Him to."

For Pam, the grieving process for Amanda in the aftermath of the fire was particularly tough. "It was very difficult to mourn for Amanda whilst trying to stay strong for Melanie. I often wonder how we coped. But we were being prayed for and God answered those prayers by giving us the grace to do what we had to do.

"I couldn't control many of the things that were happening to my family, but I was in control of my attitude and I wanted to keep a right attitude with God about my circumstances. I was in this situation and I decided that with

God's help I would make the best of it for all our sakes."

The uncertainty over Melanie wasn't resolved quickly. And it wasn't easy for Pam to stay strong.

"We weren't sure in the beginning if Melanie was going to make it or not, but it helped her greatly that she didn't inhale any smoke into her lungs.

"I cried a lot – I still do but not as much. It's my way of releasing tension. I'd try and hold it together in front of Melanie but then just cry it all out when we left her."

Seeing what Melanie was going through in the hospital was distressing for Pam who says "She started to go to theatre on a weekly basis. She had to be held onto the theatre trolley. She knew only too well what was about to happen. They were the hardest days of my life. To see your child suffer week after week, month after month, year after year was awful.

"Getting the dressings changed was another ordeal. The pain that Melanie endured was almost unbearable to watch. Someone said to me one time 'I suppose she gets used to it.'

"But you never get used to pain at that level."

Melanie's injuries were so extensive that the surgery seemed never ending and the hospital became the little child's second home. Her parents spent countless long days in the hospital with her. And Melanie wasn't allowed visitors apart from William and Pam.

"That was because of the risk of infection" says Melanie's Mum "So we had to do it alone. Her theatre day was on a Tuesday and afterwards Melanie would be heavily sedated for up to 48 hours"

Melanie's parents took that opportunity to return home to Fermanagh and for Pam, it also gave her the chance to attend a prayer meeting every Tuesday night. "It was good to get to that to get built up again spiritually" she says.

In Belfast, the Grimsleys were able to stay with William's sister and her husband who had a home in the city. "It was a real blessing for us to be so near the hospital. Of course, we had no car and had to depend on friends and family for lifts."

Melanie's plastic surgeon was Roy Millar who was to prove to be an invaluable rock for the family.

Pam says" Roy Millar is a very gentle and gracious man. It was a blessing to have Melanie in his care. They had a very good relationship. I trusted him completely in the care and treatment he was giving her. The whole medical team were so supportive and played a big part in all of our recovery."

Another man who, of course, played a huge part in Melanie's life was her life-saver Oliver Quinn, the shy hero who pulled her from the inferno.

"Quite simply, we owe Melanie's life to him. He put his own safety on the line when he rescued her. He is a quiet and gentle man and he has a special place in all of our hearts." says Pam who admits that in the early stages of Melanie's recovery, her own emotional strength was limited.

"I could only deal with it all one day at a time. So I suppose when Mr. Millar was telling us about his plans for Mel's surgery I was probably struggling to comprehend all that was being said and explained."

But the Grimsleys took comfort and strength from their daughter. Her Mum says "Melanie was a great wee fighter and as the days turned to weeks and months her personality began to shine through and she won many hearts in and out of hospital.

"The people of Northern Ireland took her to their hearts and she became a minor celebrity. To support someone when they are in a difficult place is one of the greatest of human kindnesses."

Melanie even adopted a bit of a 'diva' attitude, says her Mum.

Once Melanie was allowed to leave the hospital and return to Fermanagh, new problems emerged as Pam suffered the agony of watching people watching her daughter.

But she says "If I was tempted to hide Mel away, she was having none of it. She enjoyed getting out and enjoying life to the full, and why not? She deserved every bit of it. I think sometimes that Melanie lost some of her childhood so to see her enjoying normal thing was wonderful."

Mel was subjected to all sorts of ignominies. Pam says she and her family were looked at, stared at, mocked and laughed at. "You name it – we've seen it."

Pam, quite remarkably, didn't, and doesn't, hold grudges. She says she knows most people didn't mean any harm. "But there is only so much that anyone can take" says Pam who went to extraordinary lengths on her outings to spare Melanie from the gawkers. She says she had to brace herself emotionally before going out the door.

"I would also make sure I sat Melanie facing away from other children in restaurants because we always had folks pointing their fingers.

"If I could have taken Mel out in the middle of the night I would have - just so that we wouldn't have to deal with other people and so that we could be a normal family for once.

"Melanie had as much right to a normal childhood as anyone else. So there was really no question of hiding her away. I suppose I was also thinking that she was going to have to learn her own coping strategies to get her through life so there was no better time to start than the present."

As Melanie grew up there were bad times a-plenty. One of the worst for Pam was when she watched as her daughter had a breakdown when she was in her last year at primary school in Kesh.

Pam says "In P7, her physical symptoms were headaches, stomach upsets and pains in her legs. At her lowest points, she was only able to walk from the bedroom to the living room. She had to use a wheelchair for outside trips and was unable to go to school. After a few months of not knowing what was wrong, Melanie began getting counselling and made a steady recovery."

Another low for Pam was the court hearing at which Melanie sought compensation for her appalling injuries. The Grimsleys went to the High Court in Belfast in 1994 for the case which is detailed elsewhere in this book.

Pam says "The court case was very difficult but I knew it had to be done. Thankfully it was settled out of court and I didn't have to go into the witness box."

Pam also had worries for Melanie in the bigger picture in the big wide world.

"When Melanie was growing up I wondered if she would be able to drive a car, hold down a job or get married.

"But she achieved all these things. Her burn injuries haven't held her back that much except she felt she couldn't go to university which was a shame. However, she is keeping up her studies at home which is the next best thing."

The clock can't be turned back but it's equally clear that Pam bitterly regrets what happened on that Saturday in Enniskillen.

"Obviously I wish with all my heart that I hadn't left the girls in my car that day, but I could not have foreseen what was about to happen. It would have been better if I had been injured. At least I had a childhood."

The legacy of the horrible accident manifests itself in unpredictable ways. For example, Pam admits there's a protective instinct within her if she spots children who are left alone in a car.

"If I see them on their own I feel like hovering about until the adults come back." says Pam who is still convinced that the fire in the car in 1988 was caused by an electrical fault in the vehicle.

Pam still has a few pictures of Amanda and Melanie before the accident. But she says "They are extremely difficult to look at. So I rarely do it"

The Melanie of today clearly fills her Mum's heart with an enormous feeling of admiration.

"As a child, she was strong and courageous with a great sense of humour and a zest for life." says Pam "She has carried those qualities through to adulthood. And to say that I am proud of her would be an understatement.

"That pride is shared by the two other daughters we were so blessed to have in the years after the accident – Elaine and Bethany."

It may seem like a contradiction but Pam says the most difficult years of her life were also her happiest. "I was just at home raising my daughters."

Pam is now, of course, a grandmother to Melanie's boys William and Leo.

She says "Melanie has a fine husband and two young sons who will grow up to support her in the years to come."

Pam is also proud of the way Melanie has been able to talk about her experiences to various church groups and other organisations around Northern Ireland as well as the fact that she has become closely involved with the charity "Changing Faces"

"Melanie's life isn't the one that I would have chosen for her. But she is opening up a trail for other people to follow. And I think that is a pretty high calling."

As for the future of her loved ones, Pam says "I hope that each member of my family will have a heart for God and allow Him to lead and guide us in all His ways. When we put Him first in our lives, He will give us everything else that we need."

Pam has written a powerful testimony about the impact that the Cornagrade Road tragedy has had on her family and her faith. It is published on a website of the Enniskillen Elim Church and in it she says that God helped her through the turmoil, though she admits that at times it was a difficult path.

And Pam confided in Melanie recently that she was finding it hard to talk about the accident and the aftermath for her contribution to this book.

But Pam says "Melanie told me that it was a legacy I could leave to help others along the way. I pray that it will."

Chapter 14

The Father's Story ...Why I Scolded Melanie After She Told Me She Wished She Was Dead

William Grimsley says his daughter Melanie has always been a fighter - right from the day she was born. For that was also the day she almost died.

"Yes, we nearly lost her not once but twice "says William. "She was born six or eight weeks premature and only weighed a couple of pounds. The medics told us they didn't think she would survive and there was nothing they could do.

"She was rushed to Altnagelvin hospital in Londonderry and they put her in an incubator - the disco lights machine, I call it. The doctors said the rest was up to Melanie.

"I can remember she was a lovely wee girl, a wee pink baby but she just turned purple.

"Our minister, the Rev Eric Moore was there every day praying for her. And there was Melanie just lying there with wires coming out of her, all over her tiny wee body.

"The machine was doing everything for her. It was a dreadful time. But Melanie was a real little battler and she fought from day one. Ten days after her birth they reckoned she would make it. She was only four pounds by then.

"It was a couple of weeks before we got her home and she started to thrive. She was a wee survivor at the end of the day and she was definitely gifted from day one. Normally a baby in her situation would have had some side effects but she came through against all the odds."

Once the worst was over William and his wife Pam thought the good times were just around the corner, with Melanie a treasured addition to their little family.

They used to take her and her sister Amanda - who was eleven months older - out for strolls in a two-baby buggy. They were as proud as punch and although money was tight for the parents, they made sure their girls wanted for nothing.

William and Pam had known each other long before they started a serious relationship. "I stopped her on the road one day" says William "She was driving a banger of a car and I asked her if she would go out with me. I definitely had a wee notion. Our first date ended up at Muckross Bay in Kesh where we had a chip."

William had been discharged from the British Army because of a duodenal ulcer. Like many other members of his family, he had served with the Royal Irish Rangers.

They were black days in Northern Ireland. " I lost a lot of friends. My brothers had narrow squeaks but luckily I didn't."

Seven months later on September 7, 1983 William, who'd earlier that year broken an ankle, proposed to Pam Noble as she was then and she accepted. Another seven months on they were married on April 7, 1984.

Amanda and Melanie made their lives even happier and they tried not to mollycoddle their second-born after her fraught arrival into their world.

"No, they both were treated the same. "says William "They were like twins. Melanie was a wee goer. Amanda was quiet and laid back."

But the Grimsley family's joy was to be-short-lived. William remembers Saturday, April 9, 1988 with clarity.

"It was a beautiful day - like summer in spring. The temperature was over 70 degrees and I'd just bought a new lawnmower. Pam's sister Stephanie had been over staying and she was going back to the bus. Pam came out to see if I wanted her to take the girls with her to the bus station and I said they would probably want to go for the spin."

William will never forget what happened next. "After Pam and Melanie went out the front door Amanda suddenly came running down the hall to give me a kiss and she said goodbye and hugged me.

"Normally I sang and whistled as I cut the grass but I went quiet and even my next door neighbour Sally commented on that. I said to her that something wasn't right. I've never said this before but I had a feeling about the way Amanda said goodbye and hugged me was just different from the way things went in the house."

Around three o'clock the phone rang. "It was from the Erne hospital and a nurse, called Sister Dundas said that Pam and the children were there. She said there was nothing to worry about, that they were okay.

"Pam had taken the car so I had no way of getting to the hospital so a friend, Maureen Brimstone offered to drive me there."

William actually passed his own fire-ravaged and still-smouldering car but didn't recognise it.

"I said to Maureen 'look at that car, that's wild' but I didn't have a clue it was my own.

"Maureen's son was in the back seat behind us and he later said he knew but he kept it to himself."

William's only thoughts were for his wife and children.

"Sister Dundas met me in the hospital and she didn't look too well. She said there'd been accident and told me Pam and Melanie were there. But she didn't mention Amanda.

"She said that there'd been a fire and in that instant I realised. I think that what happened in the house that morning with Amanda had prepared me. I sort of knew.

"The nurse asked me if I wasn't going to inquire about Amanda but I said I didn't have to. She then told me Amanda was dead.

"Her body was obviously still in the car when I passed it and they told me Melanie had got out but she was badly burnt.

"Pam came running in and she was crying and saying it was her fault but nobody was to blame.

"Melanie for some reason got out of the back seat and got into the front seat. I believe that was the reason she survived.

"They wouldn't let me see Melanie and they wouldn't let me identify Amanda. My sister-in-law who's a nurse identified her body."

For a second time in the same hospital, William thought Melanie - who had nearly died two years earlier - wasn't going to pull through.

"We didn't believe she was going to make it until the Sunday morning. They'd rushed her to hospital in Belfast. Melanie was to prove us all wrong and she did survive."

Contacting relatives and friends that sad Saturday was a nightmare. Family minister and friend the Rev Eric Moore was opening a new church in Lisburn and police interrupted the service.

"My family were watching the Grand National in a pub in Irvinestown and the RUC went in to break the news to them"

The news was bad but several papers made it out to be even worse than it was.

Reports claimed the fire wasn't an accident and that it was a deliberate attack on the car because of the political conflict at the time.

"I never thought it was a bomb" says William "I was out of the army and then the talk was that it that petrol from my new lawnmower was in some way responsible. But the machine was electric."

The reports only heightened the sense of pain for the Grimsley family whose emotions were torn between their grieving for Amanda and their prayers that Melanie might survive.

"Her face was all gone - her hair, ears and nose and hands were completely burned. They were just stumps but the only good thing was a burns specialist had happened to be in the hospital when Melanie was brought in. He accompanied her to the Royal in Belfast in the ambulance and I was told it was touch and go during the journey.

"The medical teams weren't hopeful and as we worried about Melanie, we also had to deal with Amanda's death and her funeral. Hundreds of people were coming to the house including reporters but we didn't want anything to do with the papers."

On the Sunday morning, rumours started to spread around Kesh that Melanie was dead. "Someone actually called to the door and told us she was gone. We rang the hospital in Belfast and they said she was hanging in there, even though she'd had a bad night.

"Pam was driven to Belfast to see her and I stayed here. I cried and decided to open the coffin because I wanted to see Amanda but there was only one wee patch of her face that wasn't burnt. "

Amanda was buried the next day. "Someone tried to count the number of cars in the cortege" says William "They gave up at 400. The service was held at Irvinestown Independent Methodist Church and it was the Rev Eric Moore's first funeral."

William who'd turned to painting and decorating as well as restoring antique furniture after leaving the Army, had actually worked on the church where they came to mourn Amanda.

It wasn't until three or four days after the appalling fire that William saw Melanie for the first time - driving to Belfast in a car which a neighbour had lent the family.

William recalls "When I walked into the hospital, I just saw this little body covered in bandages from head to toe. I could just see her two wee eyes and her arms were sticking up."

Consultant plastic surgeon Roy Millar didn't try to gloss over the horrific scenario.

William says "He sat us down and told us that he had never seen anyone as bad and still surviving.

"He said he planned to remove Melanie's ears, nose and all her digits sooner than later. He said there was no hair or flesh on her head - apart from a hairline at the back of her head where the fire never touched.

"We were informed that the vest Melanie was wearing on the day of the accident was fire retardant and the flames didn't go through it which meant there were no barns to her stomach and her back. But her leg was burnt."

Mr Millar said Melanie faced a complete change of life and he set out what he was going to do for her.

"He said she wasn't out of danger but they were trying to stabilize her.

"She had no lips and her nose was burnt off mostly. They had to keep carrying out operations on her and they could last between five and seven hours a time. Every day there was a battle with Melanie and it seemed like there was always something different.

"Mr Millar however was a true, true gentleman. He was with her for eleven years of her life. Anything he could do for her, he did it."

Melanie's parents received counselling to help them deal with the trauma of seeing their daughter not only without her bandages but also without her clothes.

"We had been warned that the Melanie we knew was dead and that we were going to be introduced to a different person. We were also trained on how to cope with Melanie's needs after she got home.

"We used to watch the nurses doing the dressings. But it was a nightmare to have to look at this wee girl sitting in what was effectively a cage in the hospital - a steel bed with sides on it.

"She just lay there like a mummy with a straw coming out of her mouth. It really was like something out of a horror picture. But I thought if she survived a few days she would live. Her fighting instincts had saved her before.

"What also helped was that she had no smoke in her lungs. The windows of the car were open and the smoke went out through them. The experts said that Amanda was probably alive for two or three minutes. Someone said it was one thousand degrees in the car."

Melanie was kept in the Royal in Belfast for 13 weeks and her parents stayed in the city with William's sister Myrtle at Stranmillis so they could be near their daughter.

"She was having an operation nearly every week" says William "They had to remove her fingers because they were infected. Later on they made her little stumps for her hands.

"She couldn't eat for months and when she came round after all her operations, it was fight, fight all the time. She was terrified.

"The hardest bit was taking her down to theatre - death row, I called it. She was roaring and crying - begging me 'Daddy don't take me down there.' The doors would open and all you could see were green coats and Melanie was crying 'Don't do it Daddy. Don't do it' It was devastating.

"I came out with tears in my eyes. It put years on me. Pam just couldn't cope with all that."

The operations were not minor ones.

"Every time she went in, you didn't know if she was going to come out." says William "There were two surgeons involved at times. Every week it seemed they were operating on her head and every week it all broke down and they had to pull off the grafts and start again.

"They stripped her of skin for the grafts and that was another of God's blessings - that she had skin or her back and belly for the doctors to take her donations from. She wouldn't have survived if that wasn't the case."

Then came the day when the Grimsleys had to take their daughter home to Fermanagh in July 1988. Back to the house where she used to live with Amanda.

"That was something else." says William "Melanie went through a bad time after Amanda's death. She asked about her. They were very close.

"I think she went through her own sad time. She left that April day with Amanda and that was the last time she ever saw her.

"We told her that Amanda was in heaven. And that she wouldn't be coming back.

"I believe Melanie retreated into a world of her own. She had a morbid time. She went totally quiet and she changed completely. She was sad"

But William looks back with pride on how Melanie managed to bounce back.

"She managed to adapt to all the surgery very quickly. During her eleven years of treatment she was a tremendous pain-bearer.

"I remember once when they took tissue and flesh from her groin to give her eyelids. The surgery lasted nine and a half hours and I was told to go away and come back.

"When I returned, Melanie was sitting up in the bed, dressed as a nurse! She was smiling even though her face was all stitched up.

"But that was Melanie. I personally don't think she knew what pain was. The only thing she couldn't take was the pain of getting the bandages off. We had to soak them in the bath and then pull off all the scabs.

"That went on for months. Me and Pam re-dressed them as Melanie was roaring the house down but they had to come off.

"We used to pray every day that the surgery to her head would take. But often when you took the bandages off the smell told you that the flesh and tissue had rotted and turned to puss.

"We had to get all that off and put on cream and a net over her wounds plus the foam and then take her back into hospital. But eventually the procedures did work."

William says that Melanie never knew any other life apart from the hospital, the operations, the dressings and the pain.

"She never knew the Melanie who existed before the fire. We never kept any photos apart from one. And we never held onto anything from Amanda apart from a straw hat that she got as a present."

Amanda would have been three years old in the week after the accident. Her aunt Stephanie who'd been visiting Fermanagh from England gave her a birthday present on the morning of the fire. The Grimsleys buried it with her.

The physical problems and the loss of Amanda weren't the only difficulties which Melanie had to face in her early life.

William says "What she saw in the mirror with the bandages off was terrible but she had no choice.

"She had to start being counselled and psychiatrists and psychologists tried to prepare her for what lay ahead in life."

It's hard for William to say it now but he admits that there were times when he was in despair over Melanie. "I used to wonder if she would have been worse with the burns or safe in the arms of Jesus with Amanda.

"But just look at her now. That's the answer"

Wiliam says he can never re-pay the medical teams who helped his daughter. One of the major breakthroughs was the invention of a plastic mask which was put on her face.

"Her face had been like a ploughed field with all the scars on it. But then came this wonderful mask. She had to wear it for 24 hours a day, seven days a week for two years. It fitted right over her face with cream applied underneath it.

"At times we had to put rulers on Melanie's arms to stop her bending her arms to scratch her face.

"And they even had to make a mask for one of Melanie's dolls as well because that was the only way that she would agree to wear it.

"There were many disagreements with Melanie. But we had to be cruel to be kind, to let her know who the boss was."

William and Pam also resolved that they weren't going to hide Melanie away after she returned to Kesh from hospital.

"Pam used to take her out in a pram around the village. People used to cross the road because they didn't want to face us and didn't know what to say. But we didn't want Melanie to be treated any different just because she'd been burnt."

The Grimsleys didn't stay in Kesh however. "Amanda had been buried from the house so the memories got too much and we moved two miles outside the village" says William." It gave us our own space without people always looking at us."

But Melanie's moods became blacker and bleaker. "She used to say that she wished she was dead. And it was difficult to tell her that she was perfectly normal because she wasn't. But any parent would go through hell for their child and we tried to persuade Melanie that she had to accept herself for what she was. I told her there was no turning the clock back and that technology would improve things for her. And the mask did help her face in that it helped even out the scars."

William's experiences with Melanie led him to help others as a counsellor.

"One kid had been set on fire by his supposed friends. But I hope I was able to help him. I pointed out what Melanie had suffered and what she'd come through." Not that it was an easy ride, as William has explained.

And he's revealed that he stood no nonsense from his daughter. "We knew we couldn't let her off any wrong-doing just because of what she had suffered. We didn't want her to be spoiled rotten and when you love and respect a child, you need respect back.

"There were times I smacked Melanie if she misbehaved, just like any other parent would do.

"When she got frustrated and angry, I used to send her down to her room to beat the life out of the pillow. 'Take it out on the pillow and not me' I would say.

"I was rough on her sometimes and I would be strict with her because I would say that there was a big world out there and we wouldn't always be there for her."

And soon it was time for Melanie to experience that big world for herself - in the classroom. But which classroom proved to be a thorny issue.

The education authorities at first wanted to place her in a special care school - because of her disfigurement.

"But there was nothing wrong with her mind" says William "And I said she should go to a normal school. I ended up in court.

"But then there was a problem over getting a bus to pick her up for school, though that was sorted out eventually."

At Kesh Primary School where another pupil was Northern Ireland football international Kyle Lafferty, Melanie excelled in every subject. "She even got involved in riding for the disabled and she played the violin" says William

"But there were major hurdles too, especially because people were staring at her and saying things about her.

"She made friends easily but there were always the questions and the looks. Inside school children learned to see Melanie for what she was but outside people would come round for a second or third look at her. Some folk even left restaurants and swimming pools after saying the most despicable things. You could understand people looking but not gawking at Melanie.

"We used to go on holiday in Portrush and people were virtually queuing up to stare at Melanie.

"We decided the only way to deal with it was to go onto television to explain that Melanie had been injured in a freak accident and we approached the BBC's Spotlight programme to make a documentary. They brought Simon Weston who was injured in the Gulf War over to see her and he tried to lift her out of her depression. "

William says that he and his wife always tried to prepare their daughter for the future by telling her the truth.

"We warned her about all the bad things that were going to happen. She knew what was ahead. We warned her that life was never going to be a cake-walk. She knew she was different and in some ways it was to her advantage that the accident happened when she was only two years old rather than when she was a teenager who was used to walking round all glammed up.

"I remember making her look in the mirror and she cried, saying 'I'm ugly, Daddy.' But I said she wasn't.

"I told Melanie there were people worse off than herself. But her reply was always 'How can there be worse than me, Daddy?' I told her she had a wonderful, beautiful heart and a good mind.

"Once, I took her to see a boy who'd lost both of his legs. 'But he has his face Daddy' she said.

"I always told Melanie it wasn't easy and it wasn't going to be easy. I told her she had a choice - to move on or die. You have got to go on and fight it."

By this stage William had had a leg amputated. "I told her I had accepted it and got on with my life and that it hadn't held me back.

"It was a long hard struggle but Melanie eventually came to terms with her lot in life. If she hadn't, she wouldn't be where she is today.

"One of the biggest problems along the way for Melanie was starting big school - Enniskillen Collegiate which was an all-girls school. There was no doubting her ability because she had passed the 11-plus which gave her the right to go there.

"She was still going to see a counsellor every week or fortnight but it was a battle from day one at the Collegiate.

"You had all these young girls with their war paint up to the hilt, picking at spots, doing themselves up, complaining about everything. They had their expensive hairstyles and their short skirts and they would head down the town looking for boys.

"But here was Mel with a wig, no fingers and a face which wasn't the norm.

"A lot of the girls had come from primary school with Melanie and they knew her but others bullied her to such an extent that we were told she could be on the verge of a breakdown. And the fact that she was top of the class a lot of the time didn't help because there was obviously a huge element of jealousy going on. "

It was quite a while before Melanie confided in her parents about what was worrying her and making her reluctant to go to school.

A series of meetings followed between the Grimsleys, Melanie's psychologist and officials from the school.

"The psychologist said there was a danger that Melanie could take her own life. I was furious and threatened court action but I walked out of the meeting feeling that if the whole thing wasn't sorted out it could put Melanie back six or seven years. "

Happily, the crisis was averted and the bullying stopped, allowing Melanie to re-set her focus back on her school work.

"She did really, really well at the Collegiate" says William "Especially for a girl who missed so much of her school life because of hospital appointments and surgery."

Throughout much of Melanie's early years, another thought dominated William Grimsley's thinking - the fire which had caused her injuries and killed her sister.

Preparations for the compensation case dragged on and on. But William also wanted to know what had caused the fire and who was to blame.

The one person he never blamed was his wife Pam." I told her that in the hospital the first time I saw here. She couldn't have done anything more. She was only popping into a shop for a couple of minutes and she left the windows open for air and she took the keys with her.

"There was talk that maybe it was spontaneous, human combustion. Then it was suggested that maybe somebody threw a cigarette butt into the car. Then it was supposed to have been matches that started it but there were no matches in the car.

"Months and months later it became obvious to the experts that the fire had to have started up in the roof of the car. The bottom part of Melanie's body wasn't burnt yet the top half of her was.

"So it didn't come from the dashboard or the seats. The injuries just weren't consistent with either of those possibilities"

William was, and still is, convinced that the blaze started because of a fault in the courtesy light on the roof of the car.

Melanie's lawyers had to decide who to sue in the court proceedings.

William had bought the car in November 1986 from the Erne Engineering Company and had it serviced by T.P.Topping and Co Ltd in Enniskillen.

They were named in the action but they denied liability.

Melanie also had to sue her parents as the owner and the driver of the Maestro which had gone on fire.

On the second day of the case, the proceedings were halted and lawyers agreed on an 'out-of-court' settlement. A confidentiality clause was signed and even to this day it restricts what anyone can say about the case or its outcome.

But William Grimsley wasn't happy with how it all turned out. And outside the court, he said it was ludicrous that Melanie had to go to court at all. He said a no blame system of compensation should be implemented.

It's also evident that he still feels aggrieved that the cause of the fire was never firmly established during the court case.

"Something started that fire. It wasn't spontaneous combustion. It wasn't a bomb, it wasn't a petrol tank exploding and it wasn't a match. It wasn't an act of God. Eventually we will know the reason .Maybe not in this life but the next."

For William the court case didn't bring closure. "For the next two years I was tormented by it all"

Melanie did, however, receive compensation. The figure still can't be disclosed but it was invested on her behalf.

For William Grimsley and his wife Pam there were good times and bad times on the horizon as their family grew in numbers but they grew apart.

"Me and Pam had decided there was a day coming when we wouldn't be here and we thought it would be nice to have brothers or sisters for Melanie. And two sisters duly arrived to supplement the Grimsley family.

"Elaine was born on May 18, 1989 and Bethany almost exactly two years later on May 16, 1991. Having the girls made a tremendous difference. They doted on Melanie. "said William.

But William and Pam started to drift apart.

"We were both saved, born-again Christians but after the court case there was a distance which started to emerge between us. Instead of pulling us together, it put a wedge in between us. I wasn't going on with the Lord. I went cold and got very bitter over the court case. Which I shouldn't have done if I was walking with the Lord.

"Pam got deeper and deeper into religion and we realised we didn't have a relationship any more so we just decided it would be best to separate and get on with our separate lives.

"We don't fight and argue and we do things together for the three girls even though we are now divorced.

"We hold no grudges. The love died and the spark went away.

"My faith was maybe not strong enough in the Lord as what Pam's was. I still believe in the Lord and my faith."

William's faith may have weakened but he says he doesn't believe either he or his family would have been able to cope without their religious convictions.

"If we hadn't had our faith at the time I personally think that some of us mightn't have been here. Some of us couldn't have dealt with the crises without the strength in our faith and the Christian people who were behind us.

"I remember there was a period in my life when I was very emotional, upset and annoyed over Amanda's death. A minister came to the door and told me he wanted me to think about Isaiah 57 Verse One about the righteous being taken away to spare them from evil.

"It meant nothing to me but I went to Amanda's grave and bawled my head off as I sat there. The words of the verse came into my mind and started to give me a whole new look at life.

"And I thought of all the awful things that might have happened to Amanda in her later life if she had fallen foul of the wrong people or if she fallen in with a bad crowd. Maybe it was a better thing for her to be taken home at the sweet age of just three years old and to be now in the arms of Jesus.

"I got up from the grave and I had the most wonderful peace and I have never looked back. "

After Pam and William separated and eventually divorced, Melanie lived with her father for a time but he says it didn't work out and she moved back with her mother.

But her contact with her Dad never faltered 'and just as before he tried to bolster her flagging confidence about herself and her looks - especially in the context of finding someone to love.

"Mel often said that no-one would want her" says William "But I always believed there was somebody for her. I thought she was spared for a reason and that she would find happiness out there."

And sure enough Brian Higgins proved him right.

"There'd been no boys in Melanie's life before. Certainly she might have fancied someone but Brian connected with her like a live wire. They seemed to connect from day one. It was as if he was there for Melanie."

For the first time in her life, Melanie had someone other than her Mum and Dad to talk to.

William quickly saw the spark in their relationship. "I think they clicked early on. He has grown up and matured just like Melanie.

"He has become his own man and he's no dozer. He's a good cub and he obviously dotes on Melanie.

"I think Melanie had her doubts that she was good enough for him"

William was every bit the proud father as he watched Brian marry Melanie and he obviously laps up the grandfather's role too.

"People assumed she couldn't have kids but it wasn't a miracle that she did. Her insides were never damaged.

"It's great to see her now. She is very happy and content. She has found peace. You've got to come to terms with yourself and deal with the problems in your life.You don't have a choice. I would love to have my two legs but I have only one and I don't miss the other one."

Melanie has been a pillar of strength for her father in his hour of need. As well as complications from his broken ankle which led to the amputation in 2000, he has also had major spinal surgeries after the discovery that he had shattered discs there.

The procedures haven't been successful.

"They put steel rods in my spine in August 2009 but it didn't work and I'm still as bad as ever with the pain in my back.

"I still try to work as a furniture restorer but I can't bend."

Ironically William now has to put into practice the advice he gave to Melanie through the worst years of her life.

"Yes, even with all the tragedies I still believe that life is what you make it. You either cave in or you get on with it. "

William's fierce pride in Melanie - and in his other two daughters - is impossible to miss.

"I don't think that many people would have survived what Melanie has had to contend with. We nearly lost her twice but just look at the pleasure she's brought into the lives of other people - and not just her family and friends.

"She inspires many, many other people with her talks all over the place. They even invited her back to the Collegiate to speak to the girls there about looks.

"She's made a life out of the life she has and Brian loves her for what she is. But you know you might as well say that Melanie was born this way.

"Life started for her at the age of two. She didn't miss her fingers because she didn't know how to use them.

"She is my Melanie. We are so alike in many ways and we've been through thick and thin together. All of us in the family will always look out for her because of what happened back in April 1988.

"At one time she wanted to die but she has brought life into the world with two wonderful children.

"Looking back, I think there was a reason and a purpose why she survived the fire. I don't think that Amanda would have survived. She was the quiet, gentle on. Melanie was a bull and she was always going to bull on.

"She's been an inspiration to many people and she's changed many lives.

"I remember she once got a letter from a woman who was a heavy drinker and who said she was going to take her own life until she saw Melanie on the television and she realised her problems weren't anything like as big as hers.

"I do believe that Melanie is a gift from God"

Part Three

By Ivan Little

Chapter 15

The Rescuers' Stories ...the Quiet Hero Who Saved Melanie and the Man Who Got Her to Hospital

Oliver Quinn had just backed a horse in the Grand National at Aintree in Liverpool on that hot April day in 1988. He can't remember the name of the horse he backed but it wasn't the 10/1 winner Rhyme 'n' Reason.

Racing enthusiasts still talk fondly of the Irish horse which became a hero that Saturday afternoon with its courageous recovery after a stumble at the mountainous Beecher's Brook the first time around to finish four lengths ahead of Durham Edition.

But there were to be other heroes many many miles from Merseyside. None greater than Oliver Quinn, a quietly-spoken self-effacing Enniskillen man whose only thought after the National was to buy a few buns for himself and his family.

He drove to the nearest shop, Rooney's on the Cornagrade Road on the western outskirts of the Fermanagh town, little thinking that he was only minutes away from making a split-second decision which was to save the life of Melanie Grimsley, a little girl he didn't even know.

Just before Oliver arrived at the supermarket, Pam Grimsley had pulled up in her husband's Austin Maestro car to buy some milk. Knowing she would be there and back in just a couple of minutes Pam left her daughters Amanda and Melanie in the car, just as a thousand mothers do day and daily.

Oliver parked his car behind the Maestro and strolled to the supermarket to buy his buns. He didn't notice the Grimsleys' car but he knows that if there'd been anything untoward, he would have seen it. Suddenly, however, the calm outside Rooney's was replaced by chaos.

Oliver says "I was in the shop for just a couple of minutes when a girl came in and shouted there was a car on fire and there were two children inside.

"I ran down and saw the shadow of someone moving in the car so I pulled the driver's door open. I saw this young girl cowering over in the corner at the passenger's window. Whether she was trying to get out or looking for some-one I don't know. I couldn't believe my eyes. It was a horrible sight.

"She was just cuddled up. There seemed to be smoke or flames coming out of her hair and her clothes.

"I just rushed in and got a hold of her by the back of the neck and pulled her out across the seat.

"I handed her over to a man who tried to put the flames out of her by rolling her on the grass. She was then driven away to the Erne Hospital. But initially I hadn't realised there were two children in the car.

"However after hearing people shouting about another youngster inside, I went back but there was no way I could get in by the driver's side.

"I went round to the back door but the handle was so hot it was like putting your hand into an oven. I got burnt but I didn't even think about it.

"However it was hopeless. I couldn't do anything. I knew that if there was anybody on the back seat, there was no way they were still alive. "

The Fire Brigade were quickly on the scene and Oliver got into his own car and drove home.

"I was very upset so I just got out of there. My daughter met me at the door and said I was as white as a sheet. I just sat down and cried. My daughter rang the doctor and he gave me tablets to sedate me.

"The police came to see me but they knew I was in no mood for talking so they asked me to come to the station the next morning"

Oliver couldn't cope in the hours that followed the tragedy.

"I only ever take a couple of pints but that night I found myself drinking and drinking. I went to bed but I couldn't sleep. So I came downstairs and drank some more and I smoked as well. I must have drunk a bottle and a half of whisky but I wasn't drunk.

"Early the next morning I walked back to the shop for more cigarettes and a car backfired as it passed me. I must have jumped four feet in the air."

Oliver went to Amanda's funeral but it was a distressing time for him. "I kept asking myself if I could have done more to save her too. I still think about it and wonder if Amanda could now be running around happy like her sister.

"For a couple of years afterwards, I kept waking up in a cold sweat. I was dreaming that I could see the whole scene again with the wee girls in the car I would wake with the sweat running out of me.

"Even now after all these years, I still think about Amanda and wonder was she lying down on the back seat?"

But friends and family have repeatedly told him to banish such thoughts from his mind, re-assuring him that he did all he could do.

Oliver was consulted by investigators trying to find out why the Grimsleys' car had gone on fire.

"I just couldn't believe how such an inferno developed" said Oliver "I walked past the car only a few minutes before it burst into flames but at that time there was no smoke, nothing. "

The nightmare of the tragedy - and the intensity and speed of the fire - still haunts Oliver "I watch the news every night but if something comes on about a fire, I have to switch over."

Oliver doesn't see himself as a hero but he's pleased to have played his part in saving Melanie.

And he's constantly amazed that people all over Ireland still remember him. He's a part-time musician who travels extensively to entertain people.

"Everywhere I go folks still come up to me and ask me if I am the man who saved the wee girl in the fire."

Oliver is proud to tell them that he did save Melanie and he also received a Royal Humane Society award for his bravery.

But it meant more to him to have Melanie and her family thank him for his selfless actions.

"I didn't know the Grimsleys before the fire but there is a bond between us now.

"The father William called with me after the accident and I went to the hospital just to inquire if Melanie was alright."

The two families have maintained their links.

Oliver says "I didn't want to intrude but I used to call out when Melanie was a baby and I bought her a wee book on her birthday after I discovered she had taken an interest in horse-riding.

"I wrote a wee message for her on the inside"

Oliver was a special guest at Melanie's wedding in 2005.

His face lights up as he recalls getting the invitation. "I met Melanie about a year before and she told me about the wedding but then I got the invite. It was like heaven."

Oliver who's a Catholic had never been to a Protestant wedding before.

"I don't care at all about what religion anyone is but I always go to Mass once a week and I was delighted to go to Melanie's church that day. It was a lovely service and something different for me."

At the reception afterwards in the Manor House Hotel at Killadeas, Oliver was surprised - pleasantly surprised - at the reaction of other guests.

"People treated me like a Lord. They were really friendly to me. And it was a huge honour when I was mentioned in the speeches and thanked for saving

Melanie. But it didn't stop there. I was asked to say something too and I was so, so chuffed."

But there were more shocks in store for Oliver after Melanie and her husband Brian decided to name their second son - Leo Oliver Higgins - after him.

"I found out even before Melanie could tell me the news. I went into a shop in Enniskillen to buy batteries and the girl behind the counter congratulated me.

"She said she'd just read in the Belfast Telegraph that Melanie had had another baby and was calling him after me.

"I can't tell you what it meant to me. I have four children of my own - the oldest is in his 30s now. I have a couple of grandchildren too and I just adore them."

Oliver who's now 70 will always be remembered as the man who saved Melanie from the awful blaze but remarkably he was also caught up in another fire tragedy in 2007.

"I was coming out of my new home to drive my daughter down to work. I saw a house on fire and a young couple were screaming and roaring that there was a child inside.

"I rushed over and a neighbour told me not to go in but I got a blanket doused in water and put it around my head.

"I went upstairs but the whole room where the child was had been engulfed in flames. I couldn't see anything and I reckoned if I went in, I wouldn't come out again.

"The seven month old child was burned to death"

For Oliver Quinn the tragedy re-awakened painful memories of the past. "It's horrible to think that two young children died in fires that I was passing.

"But at least I can comfort myself with the knowledge that I was able to save someone and that someone, Melanie, is living life to the full."

For years, the identity of the man who drove Melanie to the Erne Hospital after the fire was a mystery.

But after an appeal in a column I write in the Sunday Life newspaper, I managed to track the driver down.

His name is Ernie Galbraith who was- and still is - a telephone engineer living in Enniskillen.

On that Saturday afternoon, Ernie who in now in his 50s was inside Rooney's shop when the fire broke out in the car park.

He says "I was on my way to work and stopped to get something to eat and before long I realised that a car was on fire. It's not something you normally see in the car park of a shop.

A Major award... Melanie's courage is recognised by
Prime Minister John Major and his wife Norma

The life-saver Oliver Quinn

Melanie's plastic surgeon, Roy Millar

The Founder of Changing Faces, James Partridge

Blossoming love. Melanie and Brian Higgins

Proud as punch... Melanie's parents Pamela and William pose with Mr and Mrs Brian Higgins

Melanie's 21st... with her sisters Bethany and Elaine (at front) and Mum and Dad

Happy family... Melanie with husband Brian and sons William (left) and Leo

Mum's the word... Melanie with Leo and William

Beauty for ashes - Melanie Joy Grimsley

The co-authors Ivan Little and Melanie Grimsley

"As I ran over I saw Oliver Quinn getting the door open and pulling a child out. I wasn't able to tell if it was a boy or a girl because the child was literally on fire. I now know, of course, that it was Melanie and I rolled her on the grass and started to beat her with what looked like a schoolbag. The flames were really intense and then the mother came out and she was hysterical, naturally enough.

"She was shouting 'that's my child, that's my child' so once I got the flames out on her daughter, I handed Melanie to her. She said that she had to get her to hospital and I put them both in the passenger's seat of my van and drove them to the Erne which luckily enough was only a couple of minutes away from the scene of the blaze.

"I remember looking at Melanie as I rushed up the road and I could see her wee hands had been burnt off. She was black from the fire and I thought there was no way she was going to live. I have never seen anything so bad in my life.

"But I still put the foot down as hard as I could and got Melanie and her mother to the hospital in just a few minutes."

Ernie tried his best to re-assure Melanie's Mum, Pam that he was going as fast as he could. "I was saying that we would be there soon but what could I really tell her to calm her down? There were no words."

At the hospital, Ernie parked his car close to the entrance. He recalls "They had no forewarning of our arrival. We went to the reception on the right hand side of the hospital entrance and a girl there called all the nurses and doctors down and they took Melanie away.

"I left immediately afterwards because there was nothing more that I could do. I stopped again at Rooney's as it was on my route back to work. The Fire Brigade were there by that time and I was told that another wee girl who'd been in the car was dead.

"There had nothing anyone could have done to save her from that fire. It was awful"

Ernie has never made himself known to the Grimsleys. "I haven't met Melanie or her Mum since. But I did get to know Melanie's husband Brian through his work. He used to work in a garage where our British Telecom vans were serviced. However I never mentioned to him who I was.

"I followed Melanie's progress in the papers and on the television. It's great to see how she has got on with her life."

Chapter 16

The Fireman's Story....the Horrific Images that
Are Still Fresh in My Mind

They weren't the words that fireman Alan Elliott was expecting to hear from Melanie Grimsley as they chatted in the church hall in the centre of Enniskillen.

They were talking about the day over 20 years earlier when Alan was one of a team of fire-fighters who tackled the blaze which so badly burnt Melanie and killed her sister.

Out of the blue, Melanie asked Alan if she could bring her sons to see around the fire station.

One of the boys, Will, is particularly fanatical about the fire service. And their fire engines. Which is somewhat ironic, of course, in the light of what happened to his Mum.

But Alan who's now watch commander in charge of Enniskillen's fire-fighters readily agreed to the visit. And in the spring of 2011, Melanie and her husband Brian took their sons Will and Leo to Enniskillen's fire station and went on a tour which ended with the Higgins family getting a ride on an engine.

"It's just as well Melanie doesn't have issues" says Brian.

It was from the same station on April 9, 1988 that an engine was despatched to Rooney's supermarket on the Cornagrade Road in Enniskillen to deal with the Grimsleys' car fire.

Alan Elliott was a comparatively new recruit to the fire service at the time.

Then, as now, the crews who work from the station on the Tempo Road in Enniskillen are retained fire-fighters. Which means they're part-time officers who hold down other jobs and who have to respond to fire calls at the drop of a hat. Or rather the bleeps of their pagers which alert them to emergencies.

The station isn't manned and fire crews have five minutes to get to the base "We are usually on the road within eight minutes of getting the call" says Alan.

But by a twist of fate the fire teams were able to get to Cornagrade even quicker than usual.

Alan explains "We'd already turned out to a call that day – a false alarm

114

where kids had been messing about - and we were just reversing back into the station when we were told to go to the shop.

"We were there in five minutes. It was a godsend really because it took five or six minutes off our normal response time.

"Our engines have six fire-fighters on them and that day a second machine was sent as well. I was on the first engine and we drove up to Cornagrade via the old roundabout which used to be there beside the Horseshoe Restaurant.

"The normal route to Cornagrade would be down by the river and up past the Erne hospital. But we went along Mill Street because we knew the fire was at the top of Cornagrade. As we were driving there we could see the fire and the smoke billowing into the sky."

Alan and his colleagues knew it was serious. They'd been informed that people were trapped in a car which was on fire.

"The ambulance was there before us. The car was well alight with a lot of flames and we set about putting them out with the hose reels.

"It quickly became evident that there was a child in the back but there we were unable to do anything. We didn't see Melanie. She was apparently already on her way to the hospital."

As well as fighting the fire, Alan and his colleagues started sealing off the area.

"When you have a car fire you have to get everybody back because the tyres can explode and bits can fly out. Everyone was conscious that there was still somebody in the car but as I say there was simply no chance of saving her."

Another of the fire crews' duties was to gather information about the blaze to help investigators to establish the cause of the outbreak.

"The car was just a ball of flames but it didn't look as if the engine compartment was burnt. It all appeared to be in the seating area."

Alan's fire engine had 400 gallons of water on board and he says that was enough to deal with any car fire.

It took the fire teams just two minutes to extinguish the flames. "But with car fires there's always a danger of the blaze re-igniting because there is so much heat in a vehicle. And obviously you have petrol or diesel in the tank and there's a lot of rubber about – so many things that will burst into flames again.

"It was our job therefore to keep the car cool"

Alan was one of the fire-fighters training a hose on the car. "I saw the wee girl in the back. It was tragic"

The fire crews stayed at the scene for over an hour, to ensure that there was no danger to the public. And the police then started their inquiries.

Alan says "I can still remember that it was a lovely Spring day. But all this was new to me as someone who wasn't that long in the job. But no matter what call you go to, the training takes over.

"However it's when you leave the scene to return home and go to bed that it all plays back in your mind and in the middle of the night it can really start to hit you.

"Nowadays, I'm glad to say things have moved on and we have counselling but back then it was left to the team of fire-fighters who were on the appliance to talk the issues out. It was just left to yourself to cope the best you could. There was a great camaraderie and you could always find someone who would talk to you over a coffee or something a little bit stronger.

"It was my first fire fatality. I'd only had a road traffic accident fatality before that"

For Alan the memories of the Cornagrade fire and other incidents still flash back, from time to time.

"I've over 27 years done now but there are still images which return. It is part and parcel of the job and it's something you live with.

"I'd been at the Enniskillen bomb too. My mother was at the Remembrance Day service but it turned out that she was fine.

"I was also the officer in charge at the fire which claimed the life of a baby in Enniskillen just a few years back. Again, we were couldn't save the child."

As for Melanie, Alan has followed her progress with interest.

"I would have seen her about the town regularly and it was great to see her getting on so well but I was never tempted to approach her for a chat.

"But my wife got to know Melanie and invited her to give a talk at the Women's Fellowship group that she runs in the Cathedral here in Enniskillen.

"I went along to help put out chairs and tables and decided to stay to hear Melanie. I sat quietly at the back and asked my wife not to let on I was there but of course she spilt the beans and told Melanie that I'd been on duty at the fire.

"We were introduced and spoke for a while. She got a wee bit emotional and I didn't want to upset her.

"Her talk that evening was very good and it was inspirational to hear how she just got on with her life and dealt with whatever came her way. She hasn't let things get her down and she obviously has a wonderful faith. The women in the audience were overwhelmed by what she had to say."

Chapter 17

The Medics' Stories...How the Doctors and Nurses Fought to Save Melanie's Life

For nurse Nuala McCarron it had been a quiet Saturday afternoon in the accident and emergency department of the Erne Hospital in Enniskillen. There'd been no patients in to the unit seeking attention. And for Dungannon-born but Fermanagh-based Nuala the lull presented her with a welcome opportunity to engage in cleaning duties, to give the department the once-over as she called it.

But Nuala knew to take nothing for granted. Almost exactly five months earlier to the very day she was on duty on a similarly quiet Sunday afternoon when all hell broke loose. She'd thought she's heard an explosion but a colleague said the 'thump' was the sound of quarrying.

However the workmate was totally wrong. What Nuala had heard was the sound of a no-warning IRA bomb exploding at Enniskillen's war memorial, causing carnage.

The first sign the hospital staff had that anything was amiss came when a UDR officer ran into A&E and grabbed a trolley before pushing it into the Erne car park to bring in a casualty.

It was the start of a procession of patients into the Erne for treatment after the Remembrance Day bombing in November 1987. Eleven people were to be pronounced dead before Nuala's day was over – a day she will never forget.

But April 9, 1988 is another date forever etched in her memory.

"It had been very quiet on that Saturday but I heard something outside in the middle of the afternoon. Because the windows in the department are quite high, we used to stand on chairs to look out to see what was happening.

"I saw what I think was an old Commer van which had enjoyed better days but in the passenger seat I spotted a woman holding what looked like a burnt doll. It certainly didn't look like a human being.

"I jumped off the chair and ran outside and the woman who'd been holding what I thought was a doll away from her body suddenly thrust the bundle into my arms and headed out again. I now know it was Melanie Grimsley's mother and from what I have learnt since I assume she wanted to leave to find out about her other daughter. However back in those early minutes in the A&E I knew absolutely nothing about what had happened or about any other casualties. I looked down at what was in my arms and saw that I was holding a baby who was totally grey and she was still hot."

Nurse McCarron's training immediately kicked in and she followed emergency procedures to call for urgent assistance and she instantly gave Melanie oxygen.

The immediate priority was to resuscitate the gravely ill child and provide her with vital pain relief.

Doctors rallied round and another nurse Sister Ethel Dundas liaised with the Grimsley family, keeping them updated about the frantic fight to save Melanie's life and trying as best she could to keep them calm.

She also arranged for police to stop the Enniskillen to Belfast bus to get the little girl's aunt Stephanie off the vehicle and bring her back to the hospital.

Nurse McCarron said the medics including anaesthetist Norman Chestnutt were remarkable in their determination to save Melanie.

There were real but unspoken fears that the little girl wouldn't survive. "But everyone in the hospital pulled out all the stops. I seemed to be constantly at the drug cupboard getting more and more medications for her. I also put cream on her burns and something inside me told me that she had a chance of pulling through.

"It was obvious that the next 48 hours were going to be crucial."

The entire staff on duty at the Erne made it their business to keep in touch with the battle to keep Melanie alive. "Everyone kept inquiring about her condition" said Nuala "Everyone was rooting for her."

Not everyone however realised immediately that Melanie's sister Amanda had died in the fire just up the road from the hospital.

"The ambulance men had taken her straight to the mortuary and then the word got round about her death" said Nuala " It was a very distressing day – especially for those of us like me who had a child around the same age as Melanie and Amanda back at home.

"But from my personal perspective on that day, I just went into a different zone. I was very focused on helping Melanie every way I could. I never gave up hope.

"And Mr Chestnutt was a real Trojan. There's no doubt that he saved

118

Melanie's life. He wasn't going to give up and he made sure she was stabilised for the journey to the Royal Victoria Hospital in Belfast. The resuscitation which was provided in the Erne was probably the major factor in her survival."

Nuala who trained at Belfast's City Hospital and started work at the Erne in 1982 said it was lucky for Melanie that the hospital was so close to the scene of the car fire.

"The driver of that old van was able to get her to the hospital in only a couple of minutes and I was able to give her oxygen immediately.

"If the fire had been in Kesh or somewhere like that, Melanie might not have made it."

Nuala McCarron admitted that she felt a sense of pride over her role in the struggle to save Melanie.

"I was only in an assistant's role to people like Mr Chestnutt but it was great to be part of the team that day."

Nuala who still works in the Erne Hospital has seen Melanie on a number of occasions.

"The first time was years ago in Irvinestown and she was still only a wee girl of four or five and I remember wondering what the future held for her. I thought it was going to be tough.

"But I know how well she has come through it all now. I decided to introduce myself to her when she came into the hospital to visit relatives and it was fantastic to see her and how she has recovered from a shocking ordeal.

"She has blossomed into an amazing woman. And it is wonderful to see her with her husband and her lovely wee boys."

But back in April 1988 there was no way of knowing for Nuala McCarron or any of the other staff at the Erne hospital what was going to become of Melanie as the decision was made to send her to the Royal hospital in Belfast for specialist treatment as her young life hung in the balance.

Sister Ethel Dundas can also remember the day of the fire clearly. She was one of the senior nursing officers at the Erne Hospital, primarily involved with administration.

"It hadn't been an overly busy day but working in a hospital is totally unpredictable just as the Enniskillen bomb tragedy showed us and I was also on duty that day.

But the first thing I knew about Melanie Grimsley and the fire was when she was brought into casualty. It was quickly apparent she was very gravely ill.

"I spoke with the consultant in charge and everything and everyone swung into action to help Melanie.

"But then her sister was brought into the mortuary and I went there. It was heart-breaking."

Sister Dundas who's from Fermanagh liaised with Melanie's family. "I remember thinking that her poor mother hadn't just lost one child with Amanda's passing but she also had Melanie to look after, thrown into tragic circumstances in a flash"

Sister Dundas phoned Melanie's father William to get him to come to the hospital.

"It was a very stressful time for the entire family. But they were very understanding especially as they had to cope with such dreadful news.

"Mrs Grimsley wanted to see Amanda but I told her it might be better to wait until the morning."

Sister Dundas who's now retired after 40 years of nursing in Belfast, Scotland and Enniskillen has watched Melanie's progress with interest.

"We were always inquiring about her when she was in the Royal and it was very encouraging to see how she managed to deal with everything because she suffered so much.

"I saw her pictures in the newspapers and on television and I have seen her from time to time in Enniskillen.

"But I never spoke to her. I didn't like to. I wanted to give Melanie her space."

Another member of the medical team that day was William Holmes who was on duty as a consultant anaesthetist.

William who's now retired but still works as a locum at the Erne says "I remember getting a call to casualty that they were bringing in a badly burnt child from a car fire. My colleague, Norman Chestnutt and I went round to casualty to discover that Melanie had already arrived. She was very distressed as you might expect. She was screaming.

"I looked at her and I could see the burns all over her face and her head and she'd lost her hair. There were also burns to her arms and hands. It was obviously a very serious situation. And I remember thinking she is going to have an awful time ahead of her.

"I knew she was going to have permanent scars because she had what we call full thickness burns. There are three grades of burns and the third – the deepest level - is full thickness which is burnt right through to the basement membrane. When that is gone you just getting scarring, you don't get regeneration of skin."

The medics' first task was to get a drip into Melanie. And that isn't an easy task with any child at the best of times. But it was even more difficult with Melanie because her arms – which are normally the best place for a drip – were so badly burnt.

"The problem is when the skin just weeps fluid, especially with a small child where there isn't that big a blood volume anyway. The need for fluid is very acute.

"We knew we would have to look for veins in her feet to get the fluid into her system. We also gave her pain relief.

"And Norman Chestnutt proceeded to integrate the baby. He put a tube into the trachea under sedation or mild anaesthesia, I can't remember which.

"But we paralysed the baby so that she could be artificially ventilated with a machine. The reason for that is that smoke inhalation is a big problem in burns cases because the smoke damages the lungs.

"So in order to ensure good oxygenation of the lungs, we need to integrate, paralyse and ventilate the child.

"My colleague then departed to the Royal sometime later with Melanie. And that was the end of my involvement with her. And I didn't see her again – apart from on television - until many years later."

That was in much happier circumstances when William went to see his daughter in a school play at Enniskillen Collegiate. For also on stage was Melanie and William remembered her in an instant, looking a lot healthier, it has to be said, than the last time he'd helped her in a real life-and-death drama.

Chapter 18

The Ambulanceman's Story ...Why I Prayed during My Race against Time to Save Melanie

Ambulance man Albert Wallace will never forget that breakneck journey. As he negotiated the twists and turns of the tortuous 80-odd mile road between Enniskillen and Belfast he drove as fast as he'd ever driven before. And at the same time, he prayed as he'd never prayed before.

For Albert who'd only been an emergency medical technician for less than four years in April 1988 knew it was a race against time to get Melanie Grimsley who was fighting for her life in the back of his ambulance to hospital in Belfast.

Albert had been on duty in the Erne Hospital, Enniskillen that Saturday afternoon when the call came through for him and his colleague Raymond Brown to go to Rooney's shop on the Cornagrade Road, a few hundred yards away.

The two colleagues had been on duty all day and their shift was due to finish around the time of that fire call.

It was to be an even longer day. And night.

Albert doesn't remember if he and his workmate had turned out to any other alerts that Saturday. But he has no difficulty remembering what happened after the call to Cornagrade.

He says "We weren't really told what was going on at first. You rarely get too much information. All we heard was that a car was on fire.

"Sometimes it can transpire that a car fire isn't as serious as feared."

But nothing could have prepared Albert and Raymond for what they were to find with that particular car...a vehicle that was completely ablaze.

"The whole rear compartment was just a mass of flames" says Albert. "Raymond grabbed the fire extinguisher from the ambulance but it was a waste of time. The fire service arrived on our heels and put out the blaze.

"We weren't immediately aware that someone had got out of the inferno but I now know that a passing motorist took Melanie and her Mum to the nearby hospital and we probably passed them on the road.

"But at the shop, we were told that another little girl was in the back of the car. We were helpless. The situation was hopeless.

"It was a heart-wrenching sight. But we retrieved the remains, put them in our ambulance and drove them the short distance to the hospital where a doctor came out to pronounce life extinct.

"I'll never forget the doctor's face. He was a pale man at the best of times but he went magnolia. All we could do was to take the body to the mortuary."

Like everyone else involved in the drama that day, Albert was deeply distressed about Amanda Grimsley's death.

But he was soon to get a chance to help save her sister's life.

"We got a call to do a transfer from casualty to Belfast. It was Melanie. A consultant anaesthetist travelled with us in the ambulance and there were also two nurses from the intensive care unit."

The journey is so engrained in Albert's memory 22 years on that he can still recall the registration number of the ambulance. "It was DIL 379 and the call-sign was Fleet Echo 7"

Albert says the Ford Transit ambulance was the quickest one available.

"I was glad because I don't think I ever drove as fast or prayed as hard in my life. The prognosis for Melanie had not been good. I just wanted to get her to Belfast as fast as I could, to give her every hope of survival"

With the blue lights flashing and the siren sounding, Albert managed to complete the nerve-wracking trip in one hour and ten minutes. "Yes, it was pretty fast driving. But we are well trained for it.

"You learn to drive as smoothly as possible. You have to read the road. Sometimes if there is a patient with a very bad fracture, you have to drive very slowly. But speed was of the essence for Melanie."

In the back of the ambulance the main priority for the medical team was administering pain relief for Melanie.

The destination was the Royal Belfast Hospital for Sick Children on the Falls Road where a specialist team were waiting to receive the gravely ill patient from the back of Albert's ambulance.

"We went to Accident and Emergency and we transferred Melanie on to a trolley and gave her over to the doctors and nurses who were on stand-by"

Albert then drove the Erne Hospital team back to Enniskillen at a more leisurely pace.

"It was a very traumatic day for everyone. We were all extremely worried but as the days and weeks went on, it became clear that Melanie was going to make it. It was a real lift for all of us to discover that she'd recovered. So thankfully it had turned out all right.

"She is a very special young lady and I've followed her progress in the newspapers and I was overjoyed to see her on the television on the day of her wedding to Brian."

Albert had seen Melanie from time to time in Enniskillen and decided to tell her his connection to her after her sons stopped to admire his ambulance. "I just had to talk to her and I think she was as delighted to meet me as I was to speak to her after all these years."

Albert who'd been involved in the emergency services' response to the Enniskillen bombing just five months before the fire tragedy is pleased that he was able to help Melanie.

"There is so much bad news involved with this job and with that day in April 1988 in particular but it's also re-assuring to know that there was a good news element in that Melanie survived and thrived."

Chapter 19

Amanda's Inquest and the Unanswered Questions

The inquest into Amanda Grimsley's death didn't provide any answers about the cause of the mystery fire which killed her and injured her sister Melanie.

It was hardly surprising. For the inquest was held less than four months after the blaze. And investigators were still trying to work out what had gone wrong.

The inquest was conducted by the Coroner Rainey Hanna in Enniskillen courthouse in the centre of the town.

And at the end of the brief hearing, the Coroner concluded that "for a reason or reasons unknown the car went on fire and caused the child's death"

But Mr Hanna also praised Oliver Quinn for his 'valiant efforts' in trying to save Amanda and for rescuing her sister.

Mr Quinn told the inquest that after hearing that a car was on fire outside Rooney's shop he thought it might be his own vehicle but on running outside he discovered it was the Grimsleys' Maestro which was engulfed in flames and thick blue smoke. He said he pulled Melanie out of the front of the car and placed her on the ground.

But after he tried to open the back door by reaching through the driver's door, he was beaten back by the intense heat.

He said he tried in vain to break the back window.

The little girls' mother Pam Grimsley told how she left Amanda and Melanie in the car and went to do some shopping in Rooney's but heard a woman shout "Oh my God. Look that car is on fire."

She said she ran out and was told Melanie had been rescued but Amanda was still inside the car.

An eye-witness Alacoque Elizabeth Rodgers said she saw a young child standing between the two front seats of the Maestro playing with the steering wheel.

She said she saw Oliver Quinn try to save Amanda after rescuing Melanie but he was driven back by the heat.

She said she too tried to save the second child by opening the back door of the hatchback. But she said the smoke was too thick and the heat too intense for any further rescue attempts to be made.

Fire officer Tony Hallett told the inquest that after the fire was put out he found the body of a young child in the back seat of the car and that he removed Amanda from the wreckage.

A pathologist's report said there was evidence of carbon monoxide poisoning but Amanda had died rapidly as a result of extensive burns.

He said the pattern of the burns suggested that Amanda was lying down at the time of the fire.

And policeman Constable Raymond Campbell said that he believed the fire had started somewhere in the rear of the car.

The Coroner extended his condolences to the Grimsley family and their solicitor Donal Fee thanked him and all the people who had been on the scene of the fire.

Essentially, no-one was any the wiser after the inquest. And for the next five years, experts worked long and hard to solve the riddle of why the Austin Maestro burst into flames without any warning.

And apparently for no reason.

Chapter 20

The Compensation Court Case ...what the Papers Said

Even by Northern Ireland's standards, Melanie Grimsley's case in the High Court in Belfast was a highly unusual one.

For Melanie who was only seven at the time arrived at the imposing Courts of Justice in Chichester Street on Monday, January 10 1994, with the very people she was suing for damages.

It was a quirk of a judicial system which demands that someone has to be to blame or liable for all accidents that she had to sue her mother and father and their insurance company because Pam was driving the car on the fateful day of that awful fire and William owned it.

Obviously Melanie was too young to take the case itself so it was her uncle Ian – her father's brother - who brought it in her name.

They also sued the Erne Engineering Company Ltd who sold William the 1984 Austin Maestro and T.P.Topping and Co Ltd, the Enniskillen garage who serviced the vehicle.

All the defendants denied liability.

Opening the case Melanie's barrister Mervin Morrow QC first talked about how she was a "very determined little girl" who'd coped well with school, getting top marks but who would need a lot of help in her adolescence.

"When you see the video of this child it will be clear that the damages should be very very substantial" he told Mr Justice Carswell.

Mr Morrow added that the fire authorities had been unable to find the cause of the fire but he said it was started by probably caused by a faulty interior light on the roof of the car.

The News Letter's Chris Thornton reported "The lawyer said Mr Grimsley had noted there were problems with the light on the day he bought the car and had subsequently tried to get it repaired.

"The light was 'an obvious, inherent danger' with a loose connection which caused a hot spot in the car, Mr Morrow said.

"He said the evidence was consistent with the roof lighting coming on fire and

dropping down as it melted on to the front seat of the car.

"That explanation was backed up by the nature of the horrific injuries inflicted on Melanie he added"

The barrister told how Pam Grimsley had gone into the Cornagrade shop in the middle of the afternoon on April 9 1988. The girls weren't strapped in but the locks were on the back doors so they couldn't be opened from the inside.

He said that the fire started within minutes and that Oliver Quinn, the man who saved Melanie, saw her crying in the front seat with her hair and clothes ablaze.

"He pulled her out through the driver's door and put her on the grass verge where someone rolled her to extinguish the flames." said Mr Morrow who told the judge that Melanie was left with virtually no facial features.

"Her nose, eyebrows, eye lashes, hair and much of her ears were seared off by the heat of the blaze which claimed the life of her sister." he said.

Melanie's hands were little more than stumps, he went on, and there was scarring on virtually all parts of her body.

But Mr Morrow also spoke of Melanie's emotional scars, with people constantly looking at her or talking about her behind her back.

The court heard that Melanie was also wary of fires and cars, especially if she thought she might be left alone.

Returning to the cause of the fire, the barrister said the evidence was that there was no cigarette lighter in the car and the vehicle's engine was not on.

He added that Pam and William Grimsley said they were not smokers at the time of the fire and there were no matches in the car.

Mr Robert McCartney QC one of the barristers for the defendants said the fire started in the back of the car rather than in the interior light at the front.

On the first day of the case reporters covering the hearing noted that Melanie looked bored. She told them "I'm okay. I like playing and I like school"

She added that she was happy and she wasn't in pain. "But I don't like people staring at me" she said.

On day two of the proceedings, it was announced that the case had been settled after overnight talks between the lawyers for Melanie and for the defendants.

The Belfast Telegraph made the story their front page lead and reported "The amount paid to Melanie Grimsley – whose face was burned off in the fire – was not disclosed. But it is understood that the out-of-court settlement is a substantial six figure sum.

"Melanie's solicitor Mr Donal Fee said outside the High Court in Belfast a confidentiality clause prevented the amount being revealed. But he added that the cash was sufficient to make provision for Melanie in the event of any future medical treatment becoming available.

"Mr Fee said that given the difficult and complex nature of the case, he and Melanie's barristers were satisfied with the outcome."

The paper added that the compensation settlement was approved by Lord Justice Carswell.

The Telegraph report went on "Despite her terrible injuries, Melanie is a happy chirpy child who has been playing with her toy pony in the hall of the High Court while lawyers wrangled over the compensation she should receive."

The News Letter devoted several pages to the settlement of the case with features on Melanie and her family as well as a report on the proceedings.

The paper reported "The cause of the blaze which gave Melanie her terrible scars remains a mystery. The long battle over compensation for her injuries was finally settled in the High Court yesterday before the facts could be decided.

"Lawyers representing the garages which sold and serviced the car, her parents and their insurers agreed to settle the case on the second day of the hearing."

Reporter Chris Thornton also wrote "The insurance took just three weeks to come through to pay for the car in which Melanie Grimsley suffered horrific burns – but it was nearly six years before the system paid for her injuries.

"The father of the tragic seven-year-old Fermanagh girl slammed the bizarre procedure which required her to sue her parents for compensation.

"William Grimsley called for changes in the law yesterday....'There's one thing that today has taught me – the system stinks.' said Mr Grimsley"

Thornton later added "Because the fire was covered by a third party fire and theft policy, Melanie had to sue her parents for the insurance money to compensate her injuries"

In a separate background piece on Melanie, the Belfast Telegraph also reported on Mr Grimsley's concerns.

Reporter Noel McAdam wrote "William, himself disabled after an accident at work, is angry that the compensation case came to court"

McAdam quoted William as saying. "It is an absolute disgrace that my daughter had to take me and her mother to court to get what in my opinion she was entitled to all along"

The paper went on to say "Mr Grimsley believes the fire started from the inte-

rior car light because it had been faulty and Amanda's and Melanie's injuries were to the upper part of their bodies.

The article said Pam suffered nightmares for years after tragedy and quoted her as saying "We still don't know exactly what happened and perhaps we never will"

The Impartial Reporter newspaper in Enniskillen also wrote about William Grimsley's anger.

It said "Mr Grimsley criticised the system where a small child had to go through the ordeal of having to go to court in order to receive compensation. He told reporters outside the courthouse there should be a 'no-fault' system for compensating injured children."

The Impartial Reporter's lengthy front page account of the court case said that Melanie had brought her action against her parents. It did not mention either of the two firms she sued, Erne Engineering or T.P.Topping.

On January 18, 1994, the Grimsleys' lawyers wrote to the paper urging them to publish a correction pointing out that Melanie hadn't issued proceedings against only her parents but also against Erne Engineering Co Ltd and T.P. Topping and Co. Ltd.

The paper's editor Denzil McDaniel replied on February 10, 1994 saying "Having fully considered this matter, we are satisfied the information contained in our report is accurate. Therefore, we do not consider it appropriate to publish the correction you have asked for"

But one section of the paper's report on the court case still resonates with Melanie. It quoted her father as saying "No amount of money will compensate for what Melanie suffered. How do you compensate a girl for what Melanie has lost? How do you compensate for Amanda my other daughter who died in the fire? There is nothing that can compensate for it."

Chapter 21

The Mystery of the Maestro Fire Which Has Never Been Solved

It's the question which everyone asks but no-one can answer – what caused the fire to ignite in the Grimsleys' car on that Saturday afternoon in April?

There are dozens of theories and Melanie's father believes the blaze was started by an electrical fault in the courtesy light inside the car.

The RUC carried out extensive investigations and one of their earliest theories was that the fire might have been sparked by a child playing with matches. But no traces of matches were found in the car and the Grimsleys were insistent that there were no matches in the car.

A report from a senior scientific officer at the Northern Ireland Forensic Laboratory in Belfast was submitted to the investigation team on July 7, 1988, three months after the fire.

Kenneth John Arnold actually carried out his probe very soon after the blaze.

In his report he said "At the request of the RUC I visited the car park of Enniskillen Police Station on April 10, 1988 where I was shown a fire damaged Austin Maestro car, registration number DIL 5113.

"The passenger compartment was completely destroyed by the fire but the engine compartment showed comparatively little damage which suggested that the fire had spread to this area."

As the fire happened during the height of the troubles – and because there had been newspaper speculation of a terrorist attack – forensic tests were carried out to find out if there had, indeed, been a link to the on-going campaign of violence in Northern Ireland.

But Mr Arnold said "The debris from the front and rear passenger areas was examined for the presence of an incendiary device such as a petrol bomb but this proved negative.

"Laboratory analysis of the debris for the presence of common fire accelerants such as petrol or paraffin oil failed to reveal anything of this nature.

"The wiring of the car was examined for the possibility of an electrical fault having caused the fire but due to the extent of the damage this could not be established."

The forensic scientist said that from the information available to him and following his examination of the car he formed the opinion that the fire was accidental.

"The fact that one child was rescued from the front of the car would tend to suggest that the fire had most probably originated in the rear portion of the car." he added.

Mr Arnold said he was however unable to determine the cause of the fire.

A scientist who had investigated car fires in the past was enlisted to help. John Butler from the College of Technology in Dublin carried out detailed tests on the car over a lengthy period of time.

In December,1985 he had written an article for a magazine called Fire Prevention. It disclosed an alarming number of car fires which had had catastrophic results right across the world.

The introduction to his article said "What have these towns around the world – Ballybay, Bexhill, Cape Town, Elsies River, Khorixas, Ladysmith, Limerick, St Helens, Skien, Vanderbylpark – got in common?

"They are some of the towns which have witnessed at first hand the horror of seeing young children trapped in burning cars and being burnt alive or seriously injured.

"The cars concerned in these fires were not involved in collisions but were parked 'safely' outside the home or a shop before the fire. Witnesses of such fires usually speak in terms of a sudden inferno and the difficulty in effecting a rescue." added John Butler.

Several case studies made for distressing reading and involved young children dying in similar circumstances to Amanda Grimsley. But just like the Enniskillen fire, the causes of many of the other parked car blazes were never determined.

In the case of the fire in Ballybay, County Monaghan Ciaran Larmer who was just four years old at the time received £200,000 under a High Court settlement in August 1988 for burns he received in April 1980.

Ciaran and two other toddlers were left unattended while the driver of the car picked up clothes from a dry cleaner's premises.

A passer-by noticed smoke and a red glow from the car's dashboard and rescued the other two children but wasn't able to reach Ciaran for several minutes by which time he had received 20 per cent burns to his face hands and thighs.

In court it was alleged that the fire was caused by a defective heating switch.

In Skien in Norway in March, 1983 a three year old girl and an eight-month-old baby were rescued by an off-duty fireman from a burning car while their mother was in a nearby shop.

In April 1984 a three year old girl was burnt to death when her father's car parked outside shops suddenly burst into flames in Bexhill, East Sussex.

In a Dublin newspaper article about Butler's report, it was revealed that a survey had been carried out of Irish parents who said they wouldn't dream of leaving their children at home without a responsible parent in attendance.

But 40 per cent said they wouldn't think twice about leaving their children in a car while doing a brief message.

Five years ago, a study in America said that over 200,000 car fires had been reported there the year before, killing hundreds of people. "The risk of a car or vehicle fire is even greater than the risk of an apartment fire. More people die in vehicle fires than apartment fires each year in the United States" said Robert Darblenet of the American Automobile Association.

A large number of the U.S.fires started in engine compartments and there were also incidents which involved occupants of cars playing with matches or lighters but the causes were largely unexplained.

The National Highway Traffic Safety Administration in America rejected claims they weren't doing enough to establish why the fires were starting. "We don't have any evidence at this point that we are missing anything" said spokesman Rae Tyson.

Back in 1989, eighteen months after the Enniskillen tragedy, a magazine called Fire Prevention carried an article by George Moore, the then Chief Fire Officer of Lincolnshire's brigade in which he spoke of his concerns about blazes in cars.

He revealed that in the UK between 1981 and 1987 there was a 32 per cent increase in accidental fires in cars and the number of blazes caused by electrical faults rose by 30 per cent.

Other causes were fuel leaks and the draining down of fuel tanks; welding or hot cutting and carelessness.

Mr Moore said fires in cars could become more serious when the upholstery in them contained flammable polyurethane foam.

He made a number of recommendations for changes to reduce the number of cars in fires.

One of them was the re-designing of the electrical fusing systems on cars and he also said that electrical wiring should be checked regularly for signs of wear or chafing.

Fire experts here and The National Highway Traffic Safety Administration in the States have acknowledged that in recent years car-makers have been building safer vehicles.

But all late too, of course, for Amanda and Melanie Grimsley and the other victims of parked car fires.

Chapter 22

The Battle Royal... How the Surgeons' Skills Helped Put Melanie Back Together Again

It took just over a minute for the raging inferno to inflict Melanie Grimsley's shocking injuries. It's taken a lifetime to fix them.

The moment Melanie was admitted to the Erne hospital in Enniskillen just after the fire, the race was on for doctors and nurses to save her life. There wasn't an overwhelming sense of confidence that she could survive but the medical team were in no mood for giving up and worked for hours to resuscitate the critically ill two-year-old and stabilise her condition, in readiness for her transfer by ambulance to the Royal Victoria Hospital complex in Belfast, where they had more extensive facilities to treat her for her appalling injuries.

Initially in Belfast Melanie was kept unconscious for 10 days hooked up to a morphine drip because medics feared her body wouldn't be able to withstand the shock and the pain.

The burns had removed skin from her head, face and arms with lesser injuries to her lower legs but she also lost many of her fingers.

After those crucially important first ten days, Melanie received her first major surgery. Skin grafts were taken from her left thigh, calf and abdomen and applied to wounds on her upper arms and her left forearm and the back of her hand.

Then under anaesthesia another problem was spotted after doctors realised she had a small abrasion of the cornea in her right eye.

Seven days later, on April 26, 1988 Melanie had skin grafts from her right leg applied to raw areas on her face after burnt tissue was removed.

More skin was taken from her abdomen and used for grafts to her right hand and forearm.

Six days afterwards, the plastic surgeons were back in action, using skin from Melanie's abdomen, chest and left calf for grafts to her scalp, face and neck.

During the same operation, what remained of the two year old toddler's fingers were amputated and skin was grafted on to her hands.

And so it went on. More surgery was performed on the 10th and 17th of

May, 1988 with grafts to her face, ears hands and right elbow.

The medics carried out more work on June 5 on Melanie's eyelids, scalp and left arm before discharging her from hospital four days later, exactly two months after the accident.

But five days later she was back under anaesthesia as a day patient to enable doctors to take a plastic of Paris mould to fashion a face mask to control scarring on her face.

But still problems persisted with the wounds on Melanie's scalp and on September 30, she was re-admitted to the Children's Hospital where five days later another skin graft from her right thigh and hip was applied to her head.

More operations followed in October to her elbow this time and she was discharged in November 29 after another couple of months in hospital.

Two months later, she was back for surgery to both hands when the tightness between her thumbs and index finger stumps was released and grafts inserted from her groin.

She was discharged on February 11, 1989 but had to return on April 3 for surgery to 'excise a tight area of scar of her upper lip and insert a full thickness graft.'

At the same time more work was carried out on her hands and she was discharged on April 11, 1989.

In September of that year Melanie had more surgery to her hands and lip during a four day spell and during a week in February 1990, there were more procedures to deal with her hands – with the middle and ring finger stumps separated.

The medics re-admitted her for six days in July as they operated on her hands and between October 15 and 23 they tried to improve the position of Melanie's ears.

Melanie had more surgery to her nose, mouth, eyes and left hand in September 1992 and she was discharged a week later and in June the following year, there were more operations to the same areas.

But eventually the major procedures came to a halt. And Melanie recently told a newspaper "When I was younger the surgery I had was because I was growing but my skin wasn't and couldn't stretch. Now that I'm not growing any more, I don't need this type of operation. I just have to accept that this is how I look"

In 2005 Roy Millar told me in an interview for a television documentary about Melanie: "She had extensive burns. About 35 per cent of her body surface was burned but more significantly were the parts of her body that were

136

severely injured. It was the whole of her face, her scalp, her ears, her hands and right up both of her arms.

" It was the sort of injury where you would not expect the child to die but at that stage it was a heart-sink thing in a way because you can project forward and think this is going to be a very disabled and a very disfigured child.

"Skin grafts were taken from unburned parts of her body. The burned tissue was removed and the skin grafts were applied. Also during that time we realised that she had lost much of the digits of both hands so she was left with a very shortened hand function.

"She had approximately one major operation per year over that period of time and it affected particularly her hands. She had many operations on both hands to try to maximise the function. Also she had surgery to her face, to her eyelids, to her nose and to her lips."

The surgeon was constantly amazed at Melanie's resilience. But he laughed as he recalled the time he heard about his patient adding a new string to her bow – literally.

Mr Millar said "Melanie herself was the sort of child who would go for whatever she could go for. I was astonished one day when her father said that she was hoping to play the violin and this was quite serious."

Thousands of television viewers including Mr Millar later realised it was no joke as Melanie appeared on the television, playing the violin alongside her friends from Kesh Primary School.

But as the seemingly never-ending procedures to reconstruct Melanie's face and hands went on, it also emerged that her eyes had been affected by the blaze too.

A consultant opthalmic surgeon who saw her compiled a detailed report for her lawyers after an examination in February 1991. He noted that extensive plastic surgery had been carried out on her eyelids which had sustained burns. The procedures were to enable Melanie to close her eyelids.

The surgeon reported that her eyelids were functioning well and her eyesight was good. However he added "Unfortunately there is no drainage of tears for either eye and there is really no prospect of surgery improving the situation here as her nose has been so badly damaged. This means that she will always have a stagnant tear film and chronic conjunctivitis.

"Because of this, her eyes are easily irritated by the sun and her lids are red and crusty all the time. Also her eyes are sticky in the morning due to a buildup of mucus in the tear film. Her eyes are watering due to the absent tear flow to the nose.

"The long term prognosis of this is, as I say, unfortunately that surgery would have little chance of improving the situation, although if her nose is reconstructed, I would feel it worthwhile attempting surgery to at least one side to see if would improve the situation. If she does not have surgery, or if surgery is unsuccessful, then I am afraid that the prognosis is that her symptoms will remain as they are now"

Melanie's tears were to flow for all the right reasons on her wedding day as her plastic surgeon Roy Millar sent a video greeting to her because he couldn't be present in person.

At the reception in the Manor House Hotel, Melanie's father William Grimsley stunned his daughter by saying "We now have a special message from Mr Millar."

The surgeon who had helped alter Melanie's life with his reconstructive skills popped up on a DVD which I'd recorded and he said: "I do want to send my best wishes to you and to Brian. We've just thinking about those years when you were in such trouble with the injury and how you came through it all and how with your determination you've got to where you are today.

"So I just want to send my congratulations to you both and my wishes and prayers for happiness for you today and also in the years ahead. I also want to send my greetings to your parents who I know stood with you and were such a tower of strength for you right through those difficult years. So bless you and we hope to hear a bit more from you later."

There wasn't a dry eye in the Manor House as the dozens of guests watched Brian Higgins hand his new wife Melanie Higgins a tissue to wipe away her tears as she listened to the unexpected words from the man to whom she owes so much.

Melanie admitted that Mr Millar's message had been a special bonus on her special day.

And afterwards with the documentary camera still running I asked her what the future held for her in terms of further surgery.

She replied "I think there does come a point when you have to say 'right this is who I am' and I have had a second chance at life so let's live it because I could spend years if I really wanted going in and out for different things and say fix this and fix my nose and fix my face. But it will never be like what it would have been"

Sitting beside her, her new husband agreed with her about her reluctance to have any more operations unless they were crucial ones. He said "I just love her the way she is. I wouldn't want to change her in any way whatsoever.

If she changed she wouldn't be Melanie anymore."

In a moving and powerful message for this book Roy Millar wrote:

No one who has sustained a deep burn injury will ever be quite the same again. The journey to recovery is often long and punctuated by many painful and traumatic experiences. When all that can be done has been done, scars remain and function may not be fully restored; and the scars are only the most visible part of the legacy, a marker for the inner emotional pain that lingers, the tearing of identity, the marring of self image, and the sense of isolation in a society in which they no longer seem to fit.

If this is true for adults, how much more in the case of a little child, frightened and without choice in the midst of one painful and bewildering experience after another in apparently unending sequence. Then the journey through adolescence begins, with disfigurement as a badge of identity that, all too often, triggers a negative reaction or thoughtless comment. As I looked at the two-year-old Melanie Grimsley in the Children's Hospital in Belfast the future seemed bleak indeed. She was expected to survive - but what kind of future could she possibly have?

Well, now we know for in this book Melanie has invited us into her life - not just the outer event but the inner world where she has wrestled with deep questions of meaning, identity, and purpose. Her prose descriptions are sometimes heart rending and her poetry, written in moments of perplexity, is both profound and deeply moving. She found her answers mainly in relationships, with family and friends, with her new family - Brian and their children, and with her Father God in a matured and tested faith.

This book is very important for a number of reasons. In the first place it is a testimony of hope. In a world where the potential for tragedy is never far away it reveals a more important truth - that what seems to be the end of a story can become the beginning of a different narrative, very different from what would have been chosen but full of purpose and meaning.

As a child Melanie was catapulted into a world of pain and loss. Her parents gave her an immense amount of support and encouragement and carried her through the early years involving very many episodes of surgery and other distressing experiences, but the ultimate outcome lay in Melanie's small and damaged hands. As she grew up and matured she decided not to be a victim of circumstances.

Her story will be a source of encouragement to others who find themselves in situations of tragic loss. In her work with "Changing Faces", created by Dr. James Partridge out of his own similar adversity as a young person, she has become a role model and friend to many.

In the second place it is a timely challenge to some of the values of our contemporary western culture that often seems drowned in a sea of triviality - the superficial issues of style and appearance and celebrity. She highlights the contrast between her own disfigurement and the anxieties of her peers over minor physical blemishes. Her perspective is both refreshing and challenging and is, of course, rooted in the higher value system of human beings made in the image of God. An inner beauty shines through the pages - "The hidden person of the heart, with the incorruptible beauty of a gentle and peaceful spirit that is very precious in the sight of God".*

Thirdly it is a great romance, a love story set in the midst of tragedy. Nursery stories, suitable for two year old girls, often end with the statement "And they all lived happily ever after". Well, it wasn't quite like that in the years that lay ahead for Melanie and her family. And yet, within all the mystery of suffering with no simple answers, an invisible hand was guiding to a good destination. Melanie has chosen for her book the title "Beauty for Ashes". I was not conscious of this when the words of a Psalm came into my mind, "He raises the poor out of the dust, and lifts the needy out of the ash heap. He gives the childless woman a home, making her the joyful mother of children". **

My clinical involvement with Melanie came to an end in 1998, as she entered her teenage years. Seven years later I was invited by Ivan Little to take part in a television programme about her wedding day with Brian. Now, I have discovered that she is the joyful mother of two boys, William and Leo.

* 1PETER 3:3-4
**PSALM 113:7&9

Chapter 23

The Psychiatrist's Report...the Little Girl Who
Surprised the Best Minds in the Business

A psychiatrist who examined Melanie in December 1993 in the run-up to the compensation court case in Belfast was surprised by what he found.

He hadn't been expecting the then seven-year-old to be quite so "warm and happy."

He did however acknowledge the multi-layered problems that the youngster had.

The first symptom he discovered was general nervousness. "Although she has never avoided a car since the incident, she is much more anxious in it" he wrote "She would never stay in a car on her own and gets anxious and apprehensive if her mother and father get out before her. She is never happy when the car is stationary and the engine is ticking over. She has become very hyper-vigilant. The least noise such as the clicking of an indicator would concern her considerably"

He added "She has also become very wary and anxious in rooms where there are open fires. The only room in her home where there is an open fire is in the parlour which the family apparently light every weekend. Melanie always makes sure that she is as far away from the fire as possible. Even if she were very cold, she wouldn't go near the open fire."

The psychiatrist also revealed that Melanie as a seven-year-old was suffering from sleeplessness. He said her sleep had become very disturbed, initially because of her injuries to her body but later because of nightmares.

"She apparently experiences nightmares in which she would scream and shout and wake up in a sweat" he wrote "Her parents would come and talk to her and she would often ask them after leaving hospital to take her into their own bedroom but they resisted that notion and they feel it has paid off. She was so restless and disturbed at night that the parents had to put sides on her bed at home to prevent her falling out of it."

The report also disclosed that Melanie had undergone major changes in her personality and that some of them were unexpected.

"Her father informed me that prior to the accident, she was shy and withdrawn and in company was inclined to cling to her mother. However since the incident – and presumably because of her lengthy stays in hospital – she is now a more open child who would talk to anybody. And she has become more independent." said the specialist.

"However she would be inclined to worry excessively and become depressed at times. She was frustrated initially that she couldn't do some of the things she could have done quite easily before the incident, such as holding things in her hands and being able to dress and feed herself.

"Her father however says that she is a very determined child and has made great efforts to overcome her physical handicaps – so much so now that she can write very well and she has been complimented in her class as being one of the best hand writers in school. She has also taught herself to ride a pony"

The fourth symptom which emerged during the examination was that Melanie had become self-conscious regarding her personal appearance.

The psychiatrist wrote "This has been natural. This has been an horrific accident and the scars are there for everybody to see. Melanie is constantly telling her parents about people looking at her and talking behind her back. This was worse when she began school initially but now they have come to accept her.

"She would be particularly self-conscious, however, if she were shopping with her mother, swimming or involving herself in other outdoor pursuits."

The report added that a fifth symptom for Melanie was her grief about the loss of her sister Amanda. It went on "Her father informed me that following the incident and even yet, she would talk a lot about her sister. She would ask questions like 'why did it happen?' and 'why not me?' When I asked Melanie about her sister she volunteered 'I think about Amanda a lot … I miss her and I miss having a bigger sister'

"She also told me that she goes to the grave quite regularly and puts flowers on it. She never goes alone however. She added 'I have one special picture of Amanda in my bedroom in my own photo album.' She told me she looked at the picture quite often.

In his conclusions however the psychiatrist had many positive things to say about Melanie. "In spite of the trauma which she has undergone, she remarkably admits to feeling better.

"And although her early life was unfortunately interrupted by this experience at two years of age, it has been fairly happy. She is considered to be a bright, inquisitive child at school and is doing well according to the teachers' reports.

"She informed me that she would like to be a jockey because she is very fond of horses but she realises this may be an unrealistic goal. She later informed me that she would perhaps be a teacher.

"One couldn't help but be sympathetic and concerned for this child, both at present and for the future. Her injuries have been horrific. She nevertheless came through the interview with me as a warm, happy child who informed me that she was glad to be alive.

"Her talk was absolutely spontaneous and frank. Thought form was normal. Her powers of concentration and recall were good and she was an intelligent child."

The psychiatrist continued "There is no doubt that this child has been in the most traumatic of incidents with horrific injuries and has been lucky to survive it. She has been remarkably courageous and is determined to live her life as normally as possible."

The specialist welcomed the fact that Melanie was attending a psychologist and had been doing so since September 1993. He recommended that attempts should be made to help Melanie to come to terms with her facial injuries and her loss of hair and the way that other people stared at her.

He also proposed that Melanie should receive help in coping with her grief and her guilt at surviving the accident.

But the psychiatrist's report showed that even experts can get things wrong because in his conclusions he warned that Melanie might miss out on many things in the future because of her injuries and her appearance – like the prospects of her finding someone to marry.

He also expressed concerns that her chances of getting employment might be limited and that she was likely to be frustrated in not being able to live a normal life and enjoy all the pleasures such as sunbathing and swimming.

But maybe the psychiatrist should have heeded his own final remarks about Melanie. Because they summed up her future to a tee.

"I found Melanie to be a very impressive child with a strong faith, determination to get on in life and a good and supportive family." he wrote.

Chapter 24

Stars in Her Eyes...How Melanie Inspired John Major, Simon Weston,
Mr Motivator, Anthea Turner and Gerry Kelly

Simon Weston's name is as instantly recognisable as his face. The Welshman is a Falklands veteran who has championed the cause of people like him with severe facial disfigurements since he was badly injured in June 1982 during the war with Argentina.

He sustained 46 per cent burns after the ship he was on - the Royal Fleet Auxiliary vessel Sir Galahad - was bombed and set on fire by Skyhawk fighters, claiming the lives of 22 of Simon Weston's 30-strong platoon.

After years of painful reconstructive surgery, Weston turned his life around and in 1994 he was contacted by BBC Northern Ireland who were making a documentary about Melanie Grimsley and other people with disfigurements.

One of the main ideas of the programme was to hear what other people with similar problems thought the future would hold for Melanie who was just eight-years-old at the time.

But Simon Weston went one step further. He travelled to Melanie's home in Kesh to meet her and the encounter proved to be inspirational, as the war hero told Fermanagh's own little heroine not to give in or give up.

The programme opened up with a marvellous shot of Melanie who wasn't wearing a wig playing "All Things Bright and Beautiful" on her piano and talking of how difficult it was to hit the right notes with her little stunted hands.

The early part of the documentary featured Melanie's mother Pamela talking about the fire in Enniskillen and Oliver Quinn telling how he rescued Melanie and how it was feared that the car was going to explode.

Pam said she knew in her heart that her other daughter Amanda wasn't coming out of the inferno alive and she told the documentary makers how difficult the next crucial hours were at the Erne Hospital as doctors and nurses fought to save Melanie's life.

The programme later showed how well Melanie had progressed since the blaze and the producers filmed her doing normal things like reading at school,

144

horse riding and enjoying herself with her family at the swimming pool but the abnormal things of her life weren't ignored.

Reporter Jeremy Adams asked her about how she felt when people stared at her.

"I think people are very rude to me" she replied "I would just like to say to them that I was burnt in a car and would you please stop staring at me."

Melanie's parents spoke of their admiration for Simon Weston long before the Cornagrade Road fire. They said they'd remembered thinking how brave he was and how he was doing a great job coming out and facing the world after sustaining his facial injuries, never imagining that he would one day arrive on their own doorstep.

But that's exactly what happened in 1994 and during his visit, the badly burned serviceman told the badly burned schoolgirl that if he could enjoy life despite the odds then so could she.

The TV cameras captured Simon sitting on the Grimsleys' sofa putting a somewhat shy Melanie at her ease immediately.

"Are you okay, lovely?" he asked her, adding "Have you got the day off school? Well, then you are the lucky one. I have come all the way over from Wales to see you."

He addressed many of Melanie's fears about the future, including - bizarrely for an eight-year-old her belief that she would never be able to drive a car. "Oh you will be able to drive a car. No problem" said Simon.

Melanie's father William then asked Simon Weston how he dealt with people staring at him. "The staring hurts Melanie terribly" he added.

Talking directly to Melanie, Simon said "I think I coped because I realised I was special and that I was more special than the people who were staring at me. Because you are different, you have to be special – the two things are so much together.

"We are in a special club, you and me. Much as they have been with you, your Mum and Dad aren't in it. Only you and me and the others who have been burned are in the special club and it's special because we smile. It's a very special thing to be able to do. And you do smile, don't you?"

At which point, Melanie gave Simon his answer, flashing him a huge smile and the pair of them laughed and giggled later in the documentary as they fed a deer in Fermanagh.

It was an extraordinary TV image as two survivors of terrifying tragedies almost a world apart shared a special moment.

Later Simon Weston told Jeremy Adams of his admiration for little

Melanie's courage. "She doesn't have to explain herself. She doesn't have to give an excuse she's injured. She just is"

He urged viewers to accept Melanie for what she was. "Let her love you and love her. She's a lovely girl. And she just cares and she deserves to be cared for – not only by her family but by her friends and by everybody else."

The programme also focused on a number of other people in Northern Ireland who were disfigured and there was also footage from a workshop where they exchanged views with a man who knows all about the problems they encountered.

Englishman James Partridge was badly burnt in a car accident at the age of 18 and he helped set up the Changing Faces organisation who represent scores of people with similar difficulties to himself and Melanie with whom he worked closely in the years after her accident.

Partridge told Spotlight that most of the psychological difficulties of disfigured people could be traced back to problems in social interaction in how they got on with someone in the pub, in the street or at a party. He added "If that causes a problem for me then I am likely to experience a lowering of self-esteem and the next encounter that I have I will find even more problematic and there is a cyclical process downwards"

Several of the older disfigured people spoke of their fears for Melanie, based on their own experiences.

One woman said "You really have to look realistically at the fact that some day she will go out and meet people of the opposite sex and she will have relationships. She will probably have aspirations to get married and maybe have kids so she is going to find difficulty in meeting a partner.

Another interviewee said "When I first saw a picture of Melanie in the newspaper, my heart really did go out to her and I thought she is in for a very rough time."

But James Partridge was prophetic in his words when he said he had no fears for Melanie's future. . "I think she has got a great life ahead of her because I sense there is a great body of goodwill and she will pick that up, she will hear it and she will respond to it.

"Yes, she will face her ups and down, no doubt about it. But I think we are entering a new era where hopefully people are not going to be judged at face value anymore and will be judged for their real selves."

Down through the years, Melanie has appeared on television and has been featured in newspapers from time to time as the media spotlight shone on her astonishing recovery.

One of the most memorable television appearances came when she was interviewed by UTV's Maria McCann in January 1989, nine months after the fire.

Melanie was a couple of months short of her third birthday at the time and the television pictures were heartbreaking and heartwarming all at once.

The extent of Melanie's injuries was captured on television for the first time and it was evident that as well as severe facial injuries, her hands were little more than stumps, particularly her left hand.

Melanie was also wearing the clear plastic mask which was designed to keep the skin grafts on her face smooth. It was strapped to her head but it was removed to allow Melanie to eat.

Her charm and her personality beamed through the camera lens and she politely asked her parents 'Please may I have a bun?" before adroitly lifting one and starting to lick off the cream!

Minutes later the toddler chided herself. "I'm making a mess." she said before rubbing her two little stunted hands together and declaring "Look at me. My hands are dirty"

Maria who looked on in amazement asked Melanie what had happened to her and she announced: "I got burned in the fire" and Maria asked her what was going to happen next to her in hospital.

She replied sweetly "They are going to make me bigger fingers – Mr. Miller is going to make me bigger fingers"

Melanie then talked about a holiday she'd had in Scotland. And she said "I was sick on the big boat. The water made me sick and I was sick in Daddy's car as well!"

Maria remembers how Melanie rode a little tricycle around the room and tried to play a toy piano before bursting into song with "London Bridge is falling down" and "Twinkle, twinkle little star"

The entertainment only stopped after a nurse called to change Melanie's bandages but the little girl with the big spirit returned to the subject of her new fingers and vowed "I'm going to play the guitar"

Maria McCann, who's now a successful public relations executive in Belfast, says she will never forget how the interview struck a chord with the public in Northern Ireland and right across the UK.

"It wasn't just seen in this part of the world "says Maria "It was picked up by ITN who ran it in their News at Ten bulletins. The phones in UTV went crazy. People were ringing up to see if they could help Melanie in any way and then the letters started arriving with cheques for her and messages of support.

"It was the first story I'd ever done which had such an amazing response from the public.

"And I can still recall how impressed I was with Melanie. She was so happy, so stoic, so brave. It was a very special story for me to report on. And I was very humbled by this wonderful little girl who held my hand during parts of the interview."

Enniskillen journalist Lily Dane who wrote the first story about Melanie's progress in that January for the News Letter in Belfast was also captivated by her spirit and her loveable character.

Lily whose father Mervyn had covered the fire for his paper,the Impartial Reporter in Enniskillen ,had heard talk that Melanie was about to get vital new surgery and went to the Grimsleys' house in Kesh.

"I remember that nothing much had been written about Melanie in the months after the fire and I went there to find that she was just a typical chirpy little toddler who just bounced about the place. Despite all her injuries she didn't seem to be too bothered by anything.

She says "I quickly discovered that underneath all the burns there was just a normal little child who was really just the same as everyone else. I've followed her milestones along the way, like her first day at school, and I know that throughout Fermanagh, there's always been a great affection and pride in Melanie, probably because she just got on with her life and achieved so many things. She's never let anything hold her back."

Lily compiled a graphic and moving account of just how appalling the injuries to Melanie's face, head and hands really were.

She also wrote that the mask which Melanie was wearing 24 hours a day in 1989 was actually her third one because every time she grew, she needed a new one.

Lily also reported that Melanie had continually called for her sister Amanda after the accident and her parents told her she was 'staying in heaven with Jesus"

For several years, newspapers and magazines followed up on Melanie's story and not just in Northern Ireland. And of course the compensation case in the High Court in Belfast attracted massive publicity in January 1994.

Just days after the case was settled, Melanie was back on the box, on the popular Kelly show on UTV. Her father William sat beside her as the chat show host Gerry Kelly at first wondered why Melanie had to sue her parents for damages. William said that was because of the legal system which pertained in Northern Ireland where liability had to be established.

William said that before the fire Melanie had been shy and reserved. "But for some reason we got a different Melanie after the fire" said William." She was more open and would talk to anyone."

Gerry then turned to Melanie and asked her if she was a bit of a chatterbox. "Yea" she replied before talking about her love of horses and one in particular she rode every week in Enniskillen which was called Misty. "I go every Thursday when school is on" she said "I'm a good horsewoman. I can trot but I can't gallop and I can't jump"

She was asked what was the worst part of everything that happened to her and she replied "When I have to go into hospital." And she said she disliked going into theatre most of all.

She said she wasn't looking forward to going back into hospital.

She told Gerry Kelly that her school-friends didn't treat her differently from anyone else but she added "Some people I don't know would look at me in a funny sort of way. It makes me a bit sad"

William said that one of the reasons he agreed to appear on the Kelly show was to try to get the message across to people that Melanie was deeply hurt by the stares.

He said that she was distressed after people stared at her in public and he revealed that on one occasion, a swimming pool emptied after he and his daughter got in. Another child had once described Melanie to her mother as a 'horrible monster'.

"How do you explain to a child that she is not a monster?" asked William.

Gerry Kelly told me that he still remembered that interview as one of the most powerful of his long-running show. "She was a stunning little girl and the reaction to the interview was quite astonishing. People were uplifted and I know that I thought Melanie was a courageous child. I've been glad to see that she has gone from strength to strength"

As for Melanie her recollections of her appearance in front of thousands of Friday viewers are limited. "But I do remember meeting John Denver" she says.

The next year Melanie was seen by viewers of UTV's School Around the Corner programme, hosted by Frank Mitchell.

Melanie was first seen playing along with four girls and a boy in the school's violin group who also danced at the same time. The tune they played was called Rock and Roll and shortly afterwards Melanie sat down on the sofa to talk with Frank Mitchell who asked her about her operations after she said she didn't find them difficult to talk about.

She added "They usually do a lot of things to me in hospital, they don't just do one thing. I usually go in on a Monday and have my operations on a Tuesday but they give me an injection and I just fall asleep and don't feel anything. But I hate injections."

The UTV host asked Melanie what she would like to do in later life and she said she would like to work with animals before she turned to the camera and became a presenter to introduce two schoolmates who sang a song.

Melanie didn't have to wait long before she was back in the limelight. In February 1996 she went to London to receive a Child of Achievement Award sponsored by the McDonalds fast food chain..

Her gong and certificates were handed over by the then Prime Minister John Major and his wife Norma together with the former Blue Peter presenter John Leslie who was still at the peak of his popularity at that time, which was several years before a sex scandal ended his broadcasting career.

Afterwards Melanie was interviewed by a TV journalist and told him she had enjoyed the day because she had met Mr Motivator and Anthea Turner plus 'the man from Blue Peter'

Shortly afterwards, Melanie was also invited to a garden party at Hillsborough Castle and presented a posy of flowers to one of the VIPs.

She had another unexpected date with Royalty in November 2007 when she addressed a conference by the Riding for the Disabled organisation in Belfast.

The Princess Royal who is the RDA'S patron was at the body's first ever annual conference to be held in Northern Ireland.

And after hearing Melanie's stirring talk, the former Princess Anne asked to meet her. Melanie said "She was lovely. I was seven months pregnant at the time and she asked me about the baby and she said she had liked my speech."

After her baby was born, Melanie and her new son William were flown to England to appear live on the ITV programme "This Morning" where she was interviewed by Eamonn Holmes' wife Ruth. "That was a great experience" said Melanie.

Chapter 25

The Headmistress Who Knew that Melanie Could Be Top of the Class

Kate Doherty knew the good and the bad times as well as the sad times as Melanie Grimsley progressed through Enniskillen Collegiate.

Melanie's first day at the school coincided with Miss Doherty's first day as Principal of the highly-regarded Collegiate and she had done her homework, so to speak, on the new girl.

She recalls that one of the first things they did was to appoint a classroom assistant for Melanie. "This was a first for us" says Miss Doherty, who's now retired "Our concern was that we would appoint someone to whom Melanie would relate and someone who would be able to provide the balance between giving essential support and encouraging independence"

The school and the classroom assistant learnt as they went along, establishing exactly where Melanie needed assistance in classes such as Home Economics and Science where cookers and Bunsen burners posed their respective problems.

"We ensured that Melanie had help in the canteen and she was allowed to leave the final class of the day a little early so that she and her belongings could be at the bus on time." says Miss Doherty who adds that the sad memories include the occasions when Melanie needed more painful surgery in Belfast, requiring long periods of recuperation.

"There were also the times when it was clear that Melanie was having difficulty with some of her peers especially on the school bus and the rare occasions when she provided a glimpse of her inner hurt and sadness.

"I certainly remember how distressed she was over the decision to postpone further hair grafting treatment and the eventual failure of the hair transplant procedures."

Like Melanie, Miss Doherty also remembers a difficult meeting which was held to discuss her educational statement in Year 13.

Speaking frankly Miss Doherty remembers "Here was a girl with so much ability and who had achieved so much, not just academically but in other areas of school life. We had marvelled at her courage as a member of the cast in a number of dramatic productions including musicals and yet I found myself facing across the table in my office a girl who seemed to have retreated within herself and who slowly, inexorably, was ceasing to engage with school life.

"I know I would not have been the only one to have been praying for Melanie at that time "

But Miss Doherty recalls that Melanie managed to pull herself out of the spiral. "Somehow the tide began to turn, so much so that at the end of the year she achieved three A Grades in her AS level examinations and went on enthusiastically into her final year at school."

The Principal's report about Melanie the person is positive too. "She was always a sensitive, thoughtful, compassionate girl and as a sixth former she did voluntary work with the elderly.

"She was also a peer educator with the 'Drug Wiser' programme which developed her presentation and team-building skills and brought her into contact with a new range of people. Added to that, she was a valued prefect in the Religious Education Department and was chosen by her peers as Form Captain in her final year at school."

Melanie also matured into an articulate speaker and skilful writer and Miss Doherty says some of her most vivid memories of school assemblies were the times when she shared her writings with her fellow pupils.

She adds "It was clear that her Christian faith did sustain her and that it was a faith that did not avoid the hard questions."

In her final year at the Collegiate, Melanie fulfilled the expectations that she would attain high grades in her A levels. But Miss Doherty realised she was having more and more doubts about going to university.

"We had always appreciated that a move to a completely new environment with no obvious support was going to be difficult for her."

However Miss Doherty recognised that Melanie's relationship with Brian Higgins was re-defining her plans. "Clearly by now Brian was very much part of the equation and their future plans were intertwined so it was not a complete shock when Melanie decided to withdraw her university application. We discussed this with her, but we knew in our hearts that she would not be moved and the decision was final.

"It was a joy to see her attain the top grades in her three A levels and then to see her launch herself into a new role at work and then into marriage and eventually into family life. My admiration for her is profound"

But Miss Doherty's links with Melanie didn't end at the school gates. For the former Principal and her ex-pupil are now side by side in a very different project.

Melanie is a part-time secretary in Enniskillen Presbyterian Church and Miss Doherty is the clerk of sessions!

Miss Doherty says "It's been a joy to work closely with her again and to give thanks for God's work in her life."

The teachers who taught Melanie Grimsley in her primary school days in Kesh have fond memories of her too. And they've admitted they learnt a thing or two from their pupil as well. What they quickly discovered that Melanie's physical problems didn't impact on her ability to study and to achieve top grades in a wide range of subjects.

"Any doubts anyone had that Melanie wouldn't be able to cope with her school work were well and truly exploded from an early age." said one teacher.

Melanie's school reports tell the tale themselves... and there's no better example than the one for the school year 1992-93, which was key stage 1 year 3.

Melanie was six-years- old and her seventh birthday came near the end of her final term. This is her P3 report word for word:

ENGLISH	Melanie reads extremely fluently and with good understanding. Her written work is always neat, tidy and well presented. She is also very confident in all her oral work.
MATHEMATICS	Melanie has worked hard all year and has made progress in all aspects of the subject, including number work.
SCIENCE	Melanie shows great interest in the subject, particularly in those areas concerned with the world around her.
RELIGIOUS EDUCATION	Not only is Melanie interested in Bible studies but she is also beginning to develop an awareness of some of the concepts involved.
HISTORY	Melanie has a good understanding of the concept of time.
GEOGRAPHY	Melanie is developing an interest in the local environment and in the people who work in it.
ART & DESIGN	Melanie's work is always beautifully illustrated and she has made good progress in the subject.
MUSIC	Melanie enjoys singing and is developing a good sense of rhythm.

| PHYSICAL EDUCATION | Despite facing physical difficulties, Melanie tries hard and demonstrates a competitive spirit. |

OVERVIEW OF PROGRESS AND ACHIEVEMENT

Melanie is a confident, enthusiastic member of the class. She has worked hard and has made good progress. She has become increasingly independent as the year has gone on and she likes to be accepted on her own merits. I am glad to hear that she's enjoyed P3 as I've enjoyed working with her and getting to know her.

SIGNED   *H Thorpe. Class Teacher. 25/6/1993.*

Chapter 26

The Husband's Story...How I Wouldn't Change a Thing about the Love of My Life

It was the image that captured the attention – and admiration - of TV viewers as Brian Higgins exchanged his vows with Melanie Grimsley at their high-profile wedding. And in the process, his tender show of love and support for Melanie epitomises the very essence of a man who genuinely can't see what all the fuss is about if and when people 'praise' him for taking her as his wife.

On her wedding day as she stood in her eye-catching dress in front of the Rev Eric Moore at the front of Enniskillen Independent Methodist Church, it was clear that Melanie was nervous. And UTV camerawoman Julia McComish, who'd spent the morning with Melanie, could sense the wedding day jitters.

Instinctively Julia zoomed right into the couple's hands and produced THE outstanding picture of the day as Brian gently and lovingly rubbed the little fingers which medical science had made for Melanie after her own digits were burnt off in the car fire 17 years earlier.

Brian assumed that no-one would see his tender gesture. But after my documentary on Melanie and her marriage was aired shortly after the ceremony it was one of the first things that viewers who saw the programme commented on.

There were also, it has to be said, the sort of patronising remarks that Brian feared as if he was doing some sort of good deed by marrying Melanie rather than taking the woman he loved to be his wife. This was clearly no mercy mission.

And Brian certainly didn't see it – or Melanie – like that. "Why on earth, should I? I am the luckiest man in the world" he says. "I love Melanie for everything that she is. I don't see the scars or the burns. I just see a beautiful woman"

The voyage which ended at the altar for Brian and Melanie started via the telephone.

Brian who is four months older than Melanie says "The first I heard anything about Melanie was when a friend asked me to contact her. I sent her a text and we've been talking ever since – well Melanie has been talking ever since!

"We didn't see each other for months and it was a long time before I discovered that her cousin was in my year at school. He told me all about Melanie, about the fire and everything. I didn't know anything about it and I'd been too young to remember it from the news or the papers.

"But that was no concern for me. We were already friends via the texts and the mobiles. We met for the first time after school in Enniskillen and I think it's fair to say that we both quickly realised we had a chance of something special between us.

"We were very young at the time – just 15 and we were both starting our GCSE years but we made time to see each other regularly after school and on Friday nights too."

Melanie was wary about Brian seeing her without her wig.

"I saw her one day after she'd had an operation and she was wasn't wearing the wig. I had to make a slight adjustment but it didn't matter to me."

In 2004, Brian popped the question at a viewpoint overlooking Derrylin which is well-known as the home for wind turbines owned by the Quinn group.

"I went down on my knee and to be honest I didn't really have any doubts that Melanie would say yes. We both knew we wanted to spend our lives together."

As Brian says, he doesn't see the burns and scars but he does see the people who stare at Melanie.

"It used to anger me more than it does now. But I did get furious as people turned to stare intently at Melanie and it would upset her. People of all ages would do it and while you can understand the natural curiosity of children, it's the adults who really should know better. Even on days out, people will take a second look. I try to ignore them and only once have I weakened and said something.

"That was on a holiday in Wales. I suppose I realised that no-one knew me there and when one person came up and stared and stared, I just turned round and snapped 'Have you got a problem?'. They cleared off."

As Melanie has already acknowledged, there were times in her teens when she was in despair and she had many, many meetings with her psychologist. Brian tried to be her rock but he did have his black days too.

"I tried to help Melanie the best I could by supporting her and encouraging her. But I got down too. How could you not? But we worked through it and we came through it."

Brian was not able to help Melanie through one major crisis in her life, however – her problems with her loss of faith.

"I was never a big church-goer" says Brian "I was brought up in the Church of Ireland and I went to my Sunday school. But I wasn't as strong as Melanie had been. She had her ups and downs with the church but she had to resolve her issues without a lot of input from me.

"I knew however that her faith was very important to her and it was a really difficult spell in her life before she re-discovered what was missing."

Brian goes to the Elim Church in Enniskillen with Melanie and their two sons, Will and Leo. "But it's more of a family thing than anything else" he says "And besides it would be impossible for Melanie to enjoy the services if she didn't have help with the two boys"

It's obvious from even the briefest of chats with Brian that he is besotted with Melanie. "I really do think she is fantastic. She's great to have come through so much in her life. And I am proud to be with her.

"Our wedding was the happiest day of my life. But it was also the quickest. It just seemed to be over in a flash."

And talking of flashes, what about the presence of so many cameras on the big day? "It didn't bother me one little bit. It was Melanie's day and I wanted as many people as possible to see her as the magnificent woman she is."

Brian was every bit as keen as Melanie to start a family. "I always knew that having children wouldn't be a problem for Melanie. And when Will came along, it was sheer bliss even though the birth was a difficult one. Leo's arrival was equally as fabulous."

The boys have never asked Melanie or Brian about her disfigurement.

"They just see her as their Mummy." says Brian "They do know that she has tiny hands and will often help her on the very odd occasion that she needs it.

"But there isn't much that Melanie can't do for herself. She drives and she has no difficulty with operating a computer. She is extremely dexterous."

Exercising the deftest of footwork, Brian neatly sidesteps any questions about the possibility of enlarging the Higgins clan but he lets it slip that Melanie would like a girl in the family ranks.

He knows that her sons are the world to Melanie. "They are her life. She wants to spend as much time with Will and Leo as she can and that is why she decided to seek part-time work rather than a full time job. The boys have brought an extra dimension of happiness into her world."

But Brian admits that he has his own formula for lifting his wife out of any blue moods she may have. "I tell her that I'll look after the boys and encourage her to find some time for herself either by going out or by having her own space in the house.

"But the low spells are very rare these days. She has sorted out most of the things that would have upset her in the past."

Looking to the future, Brian has high hopes for Melanie and his family. The only potential blot on the distant landscape is how his sons will handle any questions from their schoolmates in the years to come about their mother.

Brian is fully behind his wife in her opposition to any more surgery. "I certainly hope there won't be any need for anything else – except, of course, if it is absolutely necessary. I know there are surgeons who would like to carry out more operations but what would be the point?

"Melanie is great as she is. She could do without the hassle of more visits to hospital and time away from the boys."

In recent times, Brian has found a new role for himself – as a Red Cross volunteer.

"Melanie spotted a poster in Kesh last year asking for people to help save lives in their communities. It wasn't a response to Melanie's situation that made me decide to sign up. I just wanted to do something positive and to find a new 'hobby' for myself, though this has turned out be like a full-time one.

"I'm part of a first responder team and we are the only one in Northern Ireland. The five of us take it in turns to be on-call. We have an oxygen kit and a defibrillator and we answer any calls for help in our area. We have a pager from the ambulance service and because we live locally, we can often be at the scenes of emergencies before the crews so it can be a matter of life or death. We also provide cover for events like festivals and bike races."

Brian won't be putting his best foot forward with Melanie's new hobby – dancing.

"There was a time when she was learning to dance for a competition. But it really wasn't my thing. So she danced with another man."

You get the sense that it'll be the only other partner she ever needs.

Chapter 27

The Aunt's Story...How the Silence Was Shattered by the Awful Truth about Melanie and Amanda

Melanie's aunt Stephanie Noble was blissfully unaware of the tragedy which was unfolding in Enniskillen on that Saturday afternoon as she travelled to Belfast on the first leg of her journey back to her home in England.

She had said her farewells to her sister Pam and her nieces Amanda and Melanie at Enniskillen bus station after a shopping expedition in the town.

"I can still remember the heat of that afternoon and I recall going to the Diamond in Enniskillen where for some reason I can also recollect there was someone playing a flute and the music seemed to appeal to Amanda" she says.

Stephanie had enjoyed her visit home and the bus journey through the familiar countryside of Fermanagh was thoroughly unremarkable as the driver went through Augher, Clogher and Fivemiletown and headed for Belfast.

It was only after the bus pulled into the Ulsterbus depot at Dungannon that Stephanie noticed anything wrong.

"I saw a car parked in the bay that our bus was coming into. And I thought that was a stupid place to park. But then I spotted that it was an unmarked police car.

"An officer got on our bus and asked if there was a Stephanie Noble on board. I was told there had been an accident and that my sister Pam wanted me home.

"I don't know why but my first thought was that Amanda had broken her leg."

In the police car however the officers said nothing to Stephanie. "Not a word" she says "I suppose they didn't know what to say or maybe they didn't know what had happened."

The trip back to Enniskillen wasn't straightforward. The police stopped en route to the town and by the side of the road the officers transferred Stephanie to another RUC vehicle. But again no words were exchanged and Stephanie clung to the belief that Amanda had a shattered limb. "I thought to myself that a broken leg can heal."

Stephanie was put into a third RUC car along the way but the officers in that vehicle were no more forthcoming than the ones in the other two vehicles.

However at the Erne Hospital in Enniskillen the silence was broken. "I was told immediately that Amanda was dead. And I was glad that no-one tried to put a gloss on it. The words were short and to the point."

It was a dreadful shock for Stephanie but there was another one to come.

Stephanie was told that Melanie had been critically injured in the fire which destroyed the Maestro car her aunt had been in, just hours earlier.

Stephanie didn't see Melanie at the Erne.

"I remember doing a lot of crying. But I told myself I should be strong. All of us were in a state of shock that day and I remember a woman approached me and asked me if I believed in healing. I told her we were a Christian family and she went away."

Stephanie didn't see Melanie until she visited her in hospital in Belfast.

Stephanie who's called Woods now returned from living in Birmingham and now calls Belleek in County Fermanagh home.

And it's crystal clear that Stephanie is proud of her niece.

"I think Melanie is a real message that the world needs to hear, especially at a time when there's so much airbrushing of pictures and when models must be thin and when there's so much emphasis on make-up and clothes.

"Melanie is a vivacious young woman who has made up her mind that she doesn't want any more cosmetic surgery; that she is who she is and people can either accept her or walk away."

Chapter 28

The Siblings' Stories…Why Melanie Is Just like Any Big Sister to Elaine and Bethany

Few people know Melanie Grimsley as well as her two younger sisters Elaine and Bethany who came into her life one and three years respectively after her older sister Amanda was cruelly taken from it.

The two girls have seen close up the struggles which Melanie has gone through to cope with the outward scars of her injuries and the inner turmoil with which she has had to wrestle down the long and difficult years. They've shared the awful times but they've also shared the happier times.

However from talking to the two girls, it's evident that they don't really see Melanie as anything other than a big sister. And like all sibling relationships, they've turned to her for advice. And they've had their squabbles and their disagreements.

But the legacy of Melanie's accident has also left them feeling protective of their sister, especially when it comes to the insensitive stares and hurtful comments from people on the street, in the café or in the swimming pool.

Happily, Elaine and Bethany stood by Melanie's side as her bridesmaids at her dream wedding in Enniskillen in 2005.

At the time Elaine said "Melanie is very strong and she copes with everything that life throws at her whether it's something to do with her burns and the way she is or whether it's to do with everyday problems. She could cope with anything."

Elaine added that she got annoyed when people stared at Melanie 'because of the hurt it caused her sister'

Bethany praised Melanie's friends – and her new husband Brian Higgins – for giving her a lot of confidence within herself.

Recently Elaine who's graduated as a secondary school teacher from Stranmillis University College in Belfast spoke in more depth about her sister but said growing up with Melanie probably wasn't as different as some people might imagine. "It was pretty similar to the experiences of other siblings" she said.

"We got on very well as children and still have a very close relationship now. I knew from early primary school about Amanda and what had happened to Melanie and I remember clearly one night crying about that shocking day in April, 1988.

"I'm not sure if this memory is from the day I first found out or not."

Elaine said she was always aware that Melanie looked different from other people but it didn't bother her, though she said she became very protective of her big sister from an early age.

"I remember staring back at people who stared at her and at times I even moved to shield her from the people who were looking at her. Even as a young child I thought people were extremely rude to Melanie.

"I could understand the curiosity of children but I expected better of adults."

Amanda's death had a profound impact on Elaine who was, and still is, a devout Christian.

She said "I think that being aware of death from such a young age helped me to mature quite quickly. I remember asking a Sunday school teacher what happened to young children when they died and being told they went to Heaven. In my innocence, I thought she wouldn't know who I was asking about.

"It was knowing that Amanda was in Heaven that first encouraged me as a child to become a Christian and the quiet strength of my Mum through her faith has encouraged me to continue as one.

"I know that without God and his sustaining power our family, and Melanie herself would have felt much worse repercussions from the fire than we currently do. That's not to say the road we travelled wasn't horrendous. And the light at the end of the tunnel was at times only a flicker but today we operate as a very normal family".

For Elaine, one of the hardest parts of her early life was not having known Amanda and realising that she couldn't share in her family's grief.

"I was however still feeling a sense of loss. It was hard to know how or when to express my feelings and to what level I had the right to. I didn't like to ask questions when I was younger but as I got older I began to understand what had happened.

"I always focussed on the effect it had on Melanie and how hard it must have been for her. But when I was in my mid to late teens I realised the impact Amanda's death must have had on my parents, not to mention the support they showed for Melanie. That they coped at all seems like a miracle to me."

Not surprisingly, some of Elaine's earliest memories are of hospitals and she can vividly remember going with Melanie to see their sister Bethany after she was born in May 1991. "Melanie was so excited and it was unusual for her to find Mum in a hospital bed instead of her." said Elaine who added that Melanie was excited to have another baby sister with whom she could play because she always loved babies and having company.

Elaine's recollections of visiting Melanie in hospital in Belfast aren't as happy and she recalled seeing her dressings being changed. "I remember thinking how awful it was for her."

Elaine, like the other members of her family, had to get used to a lot of attention surrounding Melanie. "I can still recall Dad telling me that reporters had come into the hospital to see me on the day I was born and that I'd actually been on the front page of newspapers. I loved reading the articles which quoted Mel as being really excited about my arrival."

The sisters' relationships through their teenage years were really no different to a thousand others. "We had the odd argument but generally we were close." said Elaine.

And then came the big day when Melanie told her sisters about the man in her life – Brian Higgins.

Elaine said "My instinctive protectiveness of Mel kicked in but after meeting him I quickly realised that Brian was a lovely person"

The wedding was another example of the huge public interest in Melanie. "Having a camera crew with us through the day was a bit strange" said Elaine "But there were also the earlier times when the BBC cameras filmed us going swimming and Mel was also on the Gerry Kelly show."

The products of the marriage were the happy couple's sons William and Leo. And Elaine said "Melanie is very settled and happy. The boys are little treasures and I'm so blessed that they have bonded closely with me."

Elaine said she still sees Melanie a lot. It's clear her admiration of her older sister is immense. "She had a lot more difficult childhood than other youngsters but she shone brighter than most.

"Sometimes people would pay Melanie lots of attention while more often than not they didn't know which of us sisters was which. That still happens now. If I tell local people my surname I almost always get asked, 'Do you know that family with the wee girl in the fire?'

"As young children it was difficult for us to understand why people were more interested in Melanie than in us. People would stop her in the street or they would send her toys.

"Obviously as an adult I fully understand and know that the attention in no way made up for the way Mel suffered."

William and Pam Grimsley never showed any favouritism to Melanie, even though they almost lost her. The parents' wisdom is acknowledged by the entire family.

Elaine said "We were all treated equally and fairly and when Mel did get attention from others, our parents explained this to us so we could understand why. This was really important and it helped me learn that while other people made a distinction, our family didn't.

"Mel herself was always very humble and gracious. A good example came when Melanie got to go to Disneyworld in Florida with a camp for children with burns.

"I was old enough to know where she was going and to know that I was missing out. My parents booked a holiday to Newcastle, Co. Down for us while Melanie was away and did everything to make it one of the most memorable breaks we've ever had. I actually remember wondering if Mel minded that she wasn't with us to enjoy herself!

"Melanie came home with loads of presents for us – and I'm sure that Mum and Dad had planned all that, which just goes to underline how great our folks – and Mel – have been.

"My parents didn't just do an amazing job looking after Melanie while grieving for Amanda. But they also did a superb job in supporting Bethany and me"

As for Bethany, who has been studying for a degree in childhood studies at Bangor University, Wales, she said she found it difficult to express her feelings about the fire tragedy. She said most of her information about that shocking day came from reading about it in newspapers and watching TV programmes about it.

And she said it was only with maturity she realised just what Melanie and her parents had come through.

"Melanie is often described as inspirational and brave and she is exactly that. But it wasn't until I reached the age that I am now that I can appreciate the true extent of that.

" It is only now that I have been through the teenage years and early adulthood and all the hardship that comes with it that I appreciatre just how much harder it would have been for Melanie with the extra difficulties and prejudice she faced and still faces today.

"As a child I never really understood. Melanie often got a lot more attention from the public and extended family while Elaine I were simply known as Melanie's sisters for the majority of the time. I remember perhaps being envious of this extra attention which of course now seems childish and silly.

"But in a way my naivety of why that happened is rather nice as it shows I never saw Melanie as anything other than normal. To me, she wasn't 'the wee girl from Kesh who was in the fire.' She was just my big sister. And I think that is the way Melanie would want me to see it. She never wanted any favours or sympathy for what happened."

Like Elaine, Bethany said she was very close to Melanie as they grew up. She looked up to her but with all siblings, there were conflicts and disputes along the way.

She added "Melanie has built a wonderful life for herself and is very happy. She has accepted what happened and learnt not to let it get in her way. She has proved that it doesn't matter what life deals you, the most important thing is the ability to pick yourself up and make the most of what you have.

"She has demonstrated the strength needed to do that on many occasions. I am proud to have her as my sister and I am privileged to have learnt at first hand such valuable lessons from her resilience."

Bethany said she'd also learnt a lot from her Mum. "Through everything she has managed to remain a wonderful mother and always put us first no matter what she might have been feeling. She never let anything get on top of her or weigh her down and she always managed to keep in control.

"She made all of our childhoods, especially Mel's, as normal as possible.

"Today she boasts a strong faith in God and I think that exemplifies her forgiving and compassionate nature. Not many people would have been able to cope with what happened.

"I'm certain it wasn't without a struggle but Mum is remarkable, inspiring and strong beyond words. If I grow into half the woman she is, I'll be happy."

Chapter 29

The Changing Faces Story ...the Battler Who Has Helped Others Come out Fighting

Changing Faces is an organisation which is all about changing attitudes. And Melanie Grimsley has become a willing, able and articulate ambassador for the group which represents hundreds of people who, like her, have facial disfigurements.

Melanie's first contact with the charity came in 1994 when the BBC Northern Ireland Spotlight team were making a documentary on her and the founder of Changing Faces, James Pantridge took part.

At the time, there was no branch of the group in Northern Ireland but Melanie maintained contact with their work via newsletters and longed for the time she could have their support in her own backyard.

In 2007, her wishes were realised as a local unit was set up and Melanie immediately volunteered to help by giving talks and by raising money for it. She has always said that helping others has helped her deal with her own problems.

Melanie has also published her thoughts on her own disfigurement on the Changing Faces website which features a clip of her as a seven year old talking about herself.

Latterly, Melanie has also recorded messages via video clips for the organisation for training workshops for teachers and students of education all over the UK.

Jane Francis from Changing Faces said "We use the first piece of a very young Melanie to increase teachers' awareness of their own unwitting ideas about a child whose appearance is seriously affected by an illness or injury like severe burns.

"The clip elicits reactions of shock and pity and the typical comments are 'What kind of a life can that poor child have ahead of her.'

"It's important to show it because one of the things that enables children to progress in school is having teachers who can envisage them doing well in the future and who can maintain high expectations for them."

Another video shows Melanie with her son William and Jane says "It enables teachers to throw out these inappropriate reactions and negative ideas about the future for any child like Melanie.

" Melanie teaches everyone working in education who 'meets' her via the video to disregard whatever ideas they may have about tragedy and the like and get on with their best teaching which means high expectations, nurturing all their pupils' hopes and ambitions, always demanding their pupils' best work and never taking pity, however kindly meant."

Jane estimates that as many as 3,000 teachers and education students have made what she calls 'a crucial discovery' through Melanie's videos.

She adds "Melanie has spoken to many people via her clips and thereby enabled many teachers to adopt a much more positive, constructive and effective mind-set when working with visible difference."

Jane is clearly an admirer of Melanie. She says "When I finally got to meet her my first and lasting impression was of an articulate and engaging young woman. She already had her first child William and I realised she was an attentive but not a fussing Mum.

"I remember noticing her hands and that she did everything with them as if they were quite okay."

Jane says that the young Melanie on the video clip is a totally different person from the more mature Melanie in later life. "When she was seven she seemed shy and reserved but perfectly clear and articulate. Now she has patently grown out of that shyness."

The Northern Ireland organiser of Changing Faces Jan Wright says Melanie has been an inspiration to countless people here.

She says "My first contact with her was in relation to a query she had about a children's burn camp with which she had been involved previously. Over time we got to know each other, albeit electronically at this stage,

"I was really struck by her determination and commitment to things she believed in. We arranged to meet for the first time when she, her husband Brian and little Will were in Belfast doing their Christmas shopping.

"We had lunch in the Marks and Spencer café in Donegall Place. I was aware of customers 'checking out' Mellie and then looking at Will. However as Will giggled and laughed with his parents, I saw the other customers starting to smile and nod over at us.

"Indeed the woman at the next table started to make conversation, asking about how old Will was, what Santa was bringing him and wasn't he a gorgeous wee boy. I think this was due in no small part to Melanie and the strong woman that she is.

"I know that she gets the second and third look all the time but she is who she is and doesn't let anything or anyone diminish that. I have huge respect for her."

Jan says Melanie has worked tirelessly as a volunteer. "She talks to a wide range of local groups and she's involved in endless fundraising for Changing Faces. She is, in essence, our voice in the Enniskillen/Fermanagh area.

"She also provides a strong voice for the organisation, participating in a number of media interviews. She always emphases her positive attitude to life and that is so much at the heart of what Changing Faces is all about.

Pat Wade of the Burned Children's Club was a beacon of hope for Melanie and showed her it was fine to be different.

Pat was a guest at Melanie and Brian's wedding and said the marriage itself would be a major boost for others with disfigurements. On the day she told me "I have never known anybody to cope with their injuries like Melanie does and to help others at the same time. It takes a lot of guts to do that and the fact that she is marrying someone today that she loves is an inspiration to children that have bad burns and feel they will never get married and never have children and families. Unfortunately that is the way a lot of them think. But Melanie getting married is just amazing and it will give them a lot of confidence to go out and take the world by storm."

The clergyman who married Brian and Melanie in Enniskillen, the Rev Eric Moore was the Grimsleys' family minister who had provided so much support for them all in the aftermath of the fire in Enniskillen.

He was proud to conduct the wedding service and proud of how Melanie had blossomed from the desperately ill little girl in the difficult days, months and years after the tragedy.

He said "She has a lovely personality and she is very caring and helpful. She has always been a joy to be with and certainly while the accident has left her with her scars, she has an inner quality which is very beautiful."

MELANIE GRIMSLEY: A TIMELINE

March 27, 1986	Born Erne Hospital, Enniskillen - premature
April 9, 1988	Car fire, Cornagrade Road, Enniskillen
April, May, June 1988	Plastic surgery procedures continue, Belfast
June 9, 1988	Discharged from hospital, two months after the fire
May 18, 1989	Sister Elaine is born
September, 1990	Starts school at Kesh Primary
May 16, 1991	Sister Bethany is born.
September 1997	Starts Enniskillen Collegiate
August 1998	First visit to Burned Children's Club Camp
November 21, 2000	Starts texting Brian
April 2001	Goes for hair surgery
June 9, 2001	Starts dating Brian
June 2002	GCSE exams
February 2004	Gets engaged to Brian
June 2004	A Level exams
August 3, 2005	Wedding day, Enniskillen
January 27, 2008	Will born
December 12, 2009	Leo born
December 16, 2009	Graduates with Administration Management Diploma
November 2011	Book is published

MELANIE'S FAVOURITE THINGS...
A TV PROGRAMME ABOUT HOSPITALS, COLIN FIRTH
AND A PINK FUNERAL

Favourite pop star:	Michael Buble
Favourite band:	Third Day who are a Christian rock band and Bon Jovi who aren't.
Favourite actor:	Colin Firth – if he wants a signed copy of this book, no problem. He's gorgeous.
Favourite actress:	Reese Witherspoon
Favourite film:	'Marley and Me' is one of my favourite films but I generally love anything girly and romantic.
Favourite TV programme:	Desperate Housewives, Strictly Come Dancing and Holby City – yes, the series which is set in a hospital.
Favourite TV personality:	Holly Willoughby
Favourite comedian:	Billy Connolly
Favourite book:	Let Me Hold You Longer by Karen Kingsbury
Favourite writer:	Janice Thompson, Cecilia Ahern and William Shakespeare
Favourite food:	Chocolate
Favourite drink:	Tea
Top holiday destination:	Anywhere with sun – I'd love to visit the Caribbean.
Favourite part of Ireland:	It's on my doorstep -the viewpoint outside Kesh over-looking Lough Erne.
Ideal car:	I would like a Kia Sportage or an Alfa Romeo Giulietta. But my favourite is my little Micra!
Biggest regret:	Not sticking up for myself more in situations where people were making me feel small.
Biggest phobias:	I am terrified of mice and birds and bats which are a sort of cross between the two.

Biggest influence on my life:	My parents
Biggest surprises for people about you:	I can't eat wheat, I would love to own a wedding dress shop and I want everyone to wear something pink to my funeral!
Biggest ambitions:	I want to look back on my life and be able to say I was a good Mum and that I helped people who were going through difficult times. I would also like to do some further studying.
Sum yourself up in five words:	Deep, emotional, girly, bubbly, feisty.
What would you do if you won the lottery?	Share it. Help people in need. Buy apartments in Belfast so people from further away would have somewhere to stay while their loved ones were in hospital. Buy myself a bigger house and a nicer car and buy my sons their own fire engine.
Where would you travel back to in a time machine?	Ancient Egypt. It's an interesting period of history and I would love to talk to some of the people who were living then.
Apart from family & friends, what couldn't you do without?	My faith and my Elemis face products.

And Finally.....

We laugh as we prepare for the photo-shoot for the cover of this book. 'It's not allowed to be a sympathy photo,' I tell Erica the photographer.

In the past newspaper photographers have composed their entire shots to show nothing but my face and in the sort of light that's made me look even worse. But I am not my face. My face is part of me. And there's a lot of personality in me, just waiting to get out.

I want people to really see me when they look at my book. And maybe as we look at my picture, I can finally say that I have been given beauty for ashes. Not only in the beauty of the life that I have now. But beauty in myself as well.

Psalm 71 v 20 (New International Version):
"Though you have made me see troubles, many and bitter, you will restore my life again; from the depths of the earth you will again bring me up."

Acknowledgements

From Melanie Grimsley

It's hard to believe that I have finally reached my goal of telling my story. Writing the book has been a challenge and there are so many people I need to thank- people who have been a key part in my story and in making my dream of a book a reality.

Firstly, I would like to thank my co-writer and friend Ivan Little for always believing in me and encouraging me to write. From the day we first met he had a vision for this book and his drive is what inspired me to write about my life to share it with others. He has been dedicated from start to finish and I would like to thank Ivan for his time and expertise. I couldn't have done this without him or our publisher Cedric Wilson who's had faith in the project from the outset. His knowledge and skills have been truly invaluable.

I wish to thank my sponsors for their contributions towards the publishing of this book. Pat Kirk Ltd in Omagh, Geoffrey Simpson from Viewback Auctions, Graham Quality Homes Ltd, First Trust Bank in Enniskillen, Trunk Flooring in Kesh and W.B. Contracts.

My heartfelt thanks go to my parents Pamela and William who have, in the most painful of circumstances, never given up hope. Their determination, support and strength have guided me through my most difficult years and they are the reason I have the courage to write. I want to thank them for picking me up when I fell, holding my hand and never letting me settle for second best.

My wonderful husband Brian has always thought I should write a book and during times when I thought it would never happen he always kept me going. I thank him for being my best friend, for growing up with me, for loving me and protecting me and for the joy he has brought into my life. His love is what lifts my spirits when times are bad and it makes the good times even better to share them with him.

I also want to thank my darling sons Will and Leo for being an unending source of light in my life; for living out the message of this book and for always accepting me for who I am. They never question, they never judge and they always love. I hope this book is something they can both be proud of in years to come.

I would also like to say a massive thank you to everyone who's made a contribution to the book which may have re-awakened painful memories for them.

There's one man, of course, I can never thank enough. And that is Oliver Quinn who rescued me from the fire, without any thought for his own life. He gave me back my life and he is - and always will be - my hero

Thanks too to Mr Roy Millar, the plastic surgeon who literally made me who I am today, taking a broken child and making me whole again in so many ways. His work has given me a face, an identity and the ability to use my hands. Without that my life would be so restricted.

His dedication and care meant so much to my family and I thank him for always fighting for me and for seeing the potential even when to others it may have looked like all was lost.

During all my years of surgery I had fantastic care and I want to say a huge thank you to all the nurses who looked after me in Knox Ward in the Royal Belfast Hospital for sick children. They became like family to me and made a difficult experience that little bit easier.

I'd also like to thank Pat Wade for showing me that it is ok to be different. Through her Burned Children's camp and her friendship I learned to embrace who I was and to follow my dreams.

My thanks go to Louise Photography in Newry who took the photo on the cover of the book. It is a beautiful photo with happy memories and I thank Louise for allowing me to use it.

For giving me my day as a princess, my thanks also go to Chantilly Lace in Enniskillen for lending me the dress for the photo shoot, to Erica Irvine for taking the pictures, to Karol Kelly for 'transforming' me for the day and to the Manor House Hotel at Killadeas for providing the magnificent backdrop for the pictures.

For helping me to complete my many hours of writing, I am also indebted to Brenda for her childcare, to Tracy for babysitting, to Presbyterian Church in Enniskillen for the use of the office and to Flo's restaurant who kept me supplied with tea!

Although my path has not been easy, God has made sure I have never walked it alone and I thank you Father for the beautiful people you have blessed me with.

I want to thank God for his unending mercy and love, for never leaving me, for protecting and guiding me. And for giving me beauty for ashes.

Footnote from Ivan Little

First and foremost, I would like to thank Melanie for asking me to help tell her story. I take it as a huge personal compliment that she had the confidence and trust in me to assist her. I would also like to acknowledge the patience and support of my wife Siofra and the help of my daughter Emma in reading the manuscripts. I'd also like to place on record my thanks to the many people who took the time to talk to me about Melanie, particularly her parents William and Pam for whom it was a difficult and at times heart-breaking revisiting of sorrowful memories.

I would also like to express my gratitude to the BBC particularly Jeremy Adams and to UTV, especially the team from the film library for their assistance. Thanks to Raymond Humphries Photography, Enniskillen;Pacemaker Press, Belfast; Below the Radar Belfast; the Belmore Court Hotel, Enniskillen and Gavin Mullan Photography, Belfast. Not forgetting the staff of the newspaper library at the Belfast Central Library, especially the ever-helpful and always smiling Brian Girvin.